Building Faith at Home

Church leaders everywhere are wrestling with how to partner with families for the spiritual development of their kids. Mark Holmen is pioneering breakthrough ideas that are tried and tested in the local church. Prepare to have your thinking stretched by his common sense and uncomplicated approach.

Gene Appel
Lead Pastor, Willow Creek Community Church
South Barrington, Illinois

When our culture went to the service economy, American families outsourced cooking, cleaning, lawn maintenance—and spiritual formation. We decided that the staff and programs at the church could take care of bringing up our children in the faith. What a colossal misassumption! Now Mark Holmen helps us understand how we can resume God conversations where we live—our homes—with the people we live with—our families.

Reggie McNeal
Missional Leadership Specialist, Leadership Network

Take whatever survey result you want; they all show we can do better with our kids . . . and we must do better!! What Mark has to say speaks right to the partnership between two of the greatest potential sources of influence in our kids' lives—the *Church* and the *family*. For the sake of your kids, please read this book and act on it as God directs.

Jim Mellado
President, Willow Creek Association

BUILDING FAITHat HOME

Why Faith at Home Must Be Your Church's #1 Priority

MARK A. HOLMEN

Regal

From Gospel Light
Ventura, California, U.S.A.

Published by Regal Books
From Gospel Light
Ventura, California, U.S.A.
Printed in the U.S.A.

Holmen, Mark.
Building faith at home : why faith at home must be your church's #1 priority / Mark
Holmen.
p. cm.
Includes bibliographical references.
ISBN 978-0-8307-4502-9 (hard cover) — ISBN 978-0-8307-4510-4 (international
trade paper)
1. Family—Religious life. I. Title.
BV4526.3.H645 2007
259'.1—dc22
2007015233

1 2 3 4 5 6 7 8 9 10 / 10 09 08 07

Rights for publishing this book in other languages are contracted by
Gospel Light Worldwide, the international nonprofit ministry of Gospel Light.
For additional information, visit www.gospellightworldwide.org.

Contents

FOREWORD

A decade ago, I was a pretty typical church leader, believing that the ministry of the local church should revolve around the needs of its adults. The theory was that if we could effectively reach to adults and help them, they would convert that investment into a moral and spiritual windfall for society.

Through a series of God-orchestrated circumstances, in 2001 I began conducting research regarding the development of and ministry to children. From the beginning of that three-year adventure, I considered it "filler"—a kind of bridge between some of the other adult-focused projects in which I was more interested. But God had other ideas. He used that project, which became the basis of the book *Transforming Children into Spiritual Champions*, to wake me up to a critical realization: What you do with children—yours and others—is the most important ministry thrust you will ever undertake.

Why? Because the moral, spiritual and relational foundations of people's lives are determined primarily by the age of 13. After that point, it is very difficult—and rare—to change those moorings. Who a person is by age 13 is pretty much who he or she will be for the rest of his or her life in terms of beliefs, values, morals, relational emphases and ideas about faith. Naturally, the Holy Spirit may intervene at any time and introduce radical transformation, but based on decades of research, I know that such deep-seated change is the exception to the rule.

That eye-opener led to a follow-up research project, which also took several years to complete, in which I studied the parenting practices in homes where the children grow up to become spiritual champions. Once again, the insights, as described in

Revolutionary Parenting, blew me away as both a parent of young children and as a leader in the church. It became apparent that even in today's culture it is possible to raise spiritual champions, but it does not happen by default; it requires the parents to be strategic and consistent in their child-rearing efforts.

Having now conducted thousands of interviews with parents and children regarding moral and spiritual development, some elements of the process have become crystal clear. For instance, the local church plays a role in the growth of children, but its involvement is not the key to success in raising godly children. The critical factor is what takes place in the home. Parents have an overwhelmingly significant influence on who their children turn out to be. A community of faith can—and should—support parents in that effort, but the responsibility and opportunity to raise God-honoring children is given to the parents.

In short, the moral and spiritual nature of every human being is predominantly shaped by his or her family experience. Parents are responsible for defining their family culture, process and outcomes. In *Building Faith at Home*, you will discover what parents and churches can do together to facilitate parents accepting and mastering the practical realities of raising Christlike young people.

For more than 20 years, our research has consistently shown that success in any transformational endeavor requires five steps be in place. First, there must be an understanding of the situation in relation to the desired conditions. Second, the leaders of the group in question must be committed to the people and to facilitating the desired outcomes. Third, there must be appropriate strategic thinking and planning that gets converted into focused actions for those outcomes to occur. Fourth, there must be sufficient resources to accomplish the job. Finally, there must be specific and measurable criteria that reflect positive outcomes, such measurement of the criteria must consistently and objectively be performed, and necessary alterations must be made to the process based on those measures.

Mark Holmen discusses these matters in this book, enabling parents and church leaders to convert good intention into good practices. Using his years of experience as both a family ministry pastor and then as a senior pastor with a special emphasis upon family ministry, he describes the various perspectives and endeavors that are needed to be a church that partners with parents as they prepare children for a life of meaning and purpose through their in-home experiences. Thankfully, this is not a book of theory; it is a volume containing practical, hands-on solutions to the challenges pastors and church leaders face in these trying times, all consistent with biblical principles and tested in the real world.

Whether or not you have young children in your home, *Building Faith at Home* addresses the most important audience your church serves: young people and their families. Use this book as another tool in your toolbox as you seek to restore the heart of our culture, the health of the local church and the vitality of the American family.

George Barna
Ventura, California
April 2007

ACKNOWLEDGMENTS

I want to acknowledge the following people whom God has used to help shape the faith at home vision in me:

To my wife, Maria, who is the true faith at home champion in our household. Thank you for being the best partner I could ever have and for supporting and encouraging me through the process of writing this book and leading this movement.

To my daughter, Malyn, who has taught me so much as her daddy! Thank you for allowing me to talk and write about our experiences together. You are the greatest gift in my life. I can't thank you enough for the way you pray for me and bless me as your father. You're the best!

To my church family at Ventura Missionary Church. Thank you for helping me to grow as a pastor and leader and for the way you have wholeheartedly supported the faith at home movement. Thank you for being the type of authentic community that allows me to follow the Lord's vision and share our experiences along the way. As a result of your faithfulness, God is clearly using us to be a light for other congregations all across the world. It is truly a privilege to serve as your senior pastor.

To my mentor Dr. Dick Hardel, who inspired and motivated me in so many ways. Thanks for your leadership, friendship and encouragement. It's been a lot of fun to see how God has led this movement forward over the years.

To my editor, Brad Lewis, who was instrumental in taking the experiences, passion and vision that God has given me and putting it all down on paper in a way that would make sense to others. Thank you, Brad, for the time and creative energy you put into this project. This could not have been accomplished without you.

To my mother, Myrne. Thank you for showing me how to love the Lord with all my heart, soul and strength in our home. Thanks for your constant love and support and for being the best example of faith-at-home living a person could ask for.

And finally, I dedicate this book to my father, Arlen, who went to be with the Lord on November 24, 2004. Dad, you touched my life in so many ways. You set an example for me in the way you joyfully served the Lord and followed His call. You truly lived your life in the way Isaiah 6:8 describes: "Then I heard the voice of the Lord saying, 'Whom shall I send? And who will go for us?' And I said, 'Here am I. Send me!'" Thank you for continuing to cheer me on from your heavenly home as I do my best to follow the Lord's leading. I love you.

Are We Up to the Challenge?

Leading a church isn't easy. I discovered that when I became a senior pastor for the first time after serving 12 years as a youth and family ministry pastor. Before long, I had people telling me that worship needed to be our top priority. Others said prayer needed to be our main concern. Some urged me to focus on preaching and teaching. Still others pushed for small groups, missions, outreach, evangelism, stewardship, youth and children's ministry.

I attended conferences, read books and listened to speakers. All made compelling arguments for why the Church needs to be seeker-friendly, purpose-driven, missional and postmodern while building believers at the same time. While all of these required important consideration, I still remained unconvinced that any of these should be our top priority.

So, if none of these are the Church's top priority, what is?

I'm glad you asked.

At a conference I attended a number of years ago, Peter Benson, director of Search Institute, made a statement that completely changed my life and ministry: "As the family goes, so goes the future of the Church. Religious life in the home is more influential than the Church."

Take a moment to consider this statement. How are families "going" today? If the future of the Church really hinges on the current health and stability of families, what does our future look like? And if religious life in the home is more influential than the Church, shouldn't we focus more of our time, energy and resources on what takes place at home rather than at church? Perhaps the most important question we can ask is this: How much time, energy and resources are we investing to make the home the primary place where faith is nurtured?

Families are struggling. Satan is strategically and methodically attacking the family unit because he knows that by destroying families, he can cause hurt, pain and alienation that will keep people away from God and the Church for generations. Studies show that prayer, Bible reading and faith talk isn't taking place in most Christian families. Because Christlike living isn't occurring in the home, families are becoming sinking ships.

I believe it is time for the Church to rescue families. Further, I believe that this can only happen by reestablishing the home as the primary place where faith is nurtured. For the past several decades, the Church has poured time, energy and resources into creating and implementing entertaining and educational programs. Yet these programs have done very little to equip parents to pass on faith to their children. Worse, the Church has created a drop-off mentality that has enabled parents to abdicate their faith-nurturing responsibility.

As a result, we find families in disarray and crisis. Families don't pray at home, read the Bible in the home, or even talk about faith together in the home. Teenagers who were actively involved as children begin to disengage as they reach their late teen or early young adult years because the faith they experienced was a program they attended at church rather than a lifestyle they lived at home.

It's time for the Church to reestablish the home as the primary place where faith is to be nurtured. It's time to make faith at home a top priority in the Church. As pastors or church leaders, we need to make a decision: Will we lead our ministry in a way that causes "parents to look after their children and children to look up to their parents" (Mal. 4:6, *THE MESSAGE*)? Or will we and our churches continue to enable a drop-off mentality through programs that temporarily engage and entertain instead of transferring and equipping?

I urge you to read on and explore the state of families today. You'll discover that what we've been doing for years through our seemingly effective programs hasn't been transferring into the home. Someone once described insanity as doing the same thing over and over again and expecting different results. If we truly want to reestablish the home as the primary place where faith is nurtured, we need to reconsider our overall approach to ministry.

So, are you ready to do something about it? In the chapters that follow, you will be armed with biblical truth and statistical data for why a faith at home-driven ministry must become a top priority in your church. You will receive a vision and practical model for how to weave faith at home into the DNA of your church. And you will learn key principles for successfully leading a faith at home movement in your congregation.

I pray God will personally give you the desire to have your church become a place that equips the home to be the primary place where faith is nurtured and that He will help you make a personal commitment to lead a faith at home-driven church.

Mark Holmen
Senior Pastor, Ventura Missionary Church
Ventura, California

CHAPTER 1 SUMMARY:

- Individuals and families often fail to apply faith or biblical living in the home.

- Satan clearly and strategically works to tear families apart.

- As the family goes, so goes the future of the Church.

- Religious life in the home is nearly extinct.

- The drop-off approach to faith often doesn't lead to lasting faith.

- Families prosper by impressing faith on their children in the home.

- Faith must be caught, not taught.

- Parents are 2 to 3 times more influential than any church program.

- During the past 40 years, programs geared toward children and youth haven't significantly helped families.

- Church leaders need to view programs through a new set of lenses.

- The problems churches face include declining engagement, loss of standing, ill-equipped parents and competition from the world.

- *Challenge*: To focus on the home as the primary place for nurturing faith.

CHAPTER 1

What Are We Accomplishing?

The local church should be an intimate and valuable partner in the effort to raise the coming generation of Christ's followers and church leaders, but it is the parents whom God will hold primarily accountable for the spiritual maturation of their children.[1]
George Barna

Nearly every time I muster the courage to set both of my feet—along with the rest of my body—on a scale, the reading ends up being completely different than what I expect. Watching my weight and following good eating habits never used to be an issue for me. But now that I'm past age 40, I've learned that something strange occurs with men and their metabolism during their middle-aged years.

I'm amazed at how quickly I can now gain 5, 10 and even 15 pounds when I simply enjoy the food I used to eat as a young adult. When I was younger, a few vigorous workouts at the gym over several days easily took care of that extra weight. Unfortunately, that's no longer the case. You wouldn't believe the number of times during the past year I've jumped into a major workout routine in an attempt to lose that extra 10 or 15 pounds.

I head off to the health club for a couple of hours each day to run on the treadmill, ride an exercise bike, work the elliptical trainer and then sit in the sauna. During this time, I'm completely confident that my rigorous and sweat-laden routine will certainly take care of my spare weight, just as it did in my younger years. At the end of the week, I'm fully prepared to see the results of my hard work. So I slowly step on the scale. To my amazement, I discover that I haven't lost 5, 10 or even 15 pounds. Instead, I've gained half a pound!

At this point, I become completely unglued. Yet in the middle of my "are you kidding me?" rant, I remember the words my wife, Maria (who, incidentally, has lost more than 60 pounds and looks better at 40 than she did when she was 20, which is completely unfair), has been saying to me: "Honey, you're not 20 anymore. If you want to lose weight, you're going to have to take a serious look at your eating habits."

What I was trying to accomplish—eating anything I want to eat and then working out a few days to take the pounds back off—simply wasn't working. The proof was in the extra weight I was carrying around. I didn't want to face this reality, yet I knew that if I didn't confront this ever-growing problem, it would only get worse.

Families in Crisis

Have you ever been in a situation like my battle of the bulge in which the true results ended up being completely different from what you thought they would be? I wonder if that's how the Pharisees felt when they expended their best efforts to thwart the movement that Jesus was leading. The apostle John records what these religious leaders did when they realized that something wasn't working: "Then the chief priests and the Pharisees called a meeting of the Sanhedrin. 'What are we accomplishing?' they asked" (John 11:47).

Notice the Pharisees focused on one question: *What are we accomplishing?* In spite of their efforts to stop Jesus, He was gaining popularity and momentum. The religious leaders of the day faced some difficult realities caused by Jesus. From their perspective, if they didn't deal with these realities, they faced some major short-term and long-term problems.

In a similar way, as pastors and church leaders we face a difficult reality that we must confront today. If we don't confront this problem, it will only get worse and we will end up facing even greater short-term and long-term issues. This problem lies at the core of many of the issues facing the Church, yet many church leaders spend little or no time addressing it and continue to go on with business as usual. While they might occasionally preach a sermon about this problem or dedicate a special evening to it, they haven't truly addressed it.

So, what problem am I talking about? Let me see if I can sum it up in 10 words or less: *Faithful Christlike living isn't happening in our homes today.*

The Heart of the Problem

In other words, families of all shapes and sizes aren't applying faith or biblical living to their everyday lives at home. They might come to church on a regular basis or enroll their children in church programs, but when it comes to talking about faith, praying together, reading the Bible in the home or doing devotions as a family, these practices simply aren't happening. The result is a crisis that leads to both short-term and long-term consequences.

As Peter Benson stated, the future of the Church will go the way the family goes. If this statement is true, we need to be asking ourselves some important questions: How are families "going" today? If the future of the Church depends on the current health and stability of families, what does our future look like?

When I began my congregational ministry, it didn't take long for me to witness firsthand that families are in crisis. The first church I served had a congregation of about 400 worshipers in a fairly affluent suburb of Minneapolis. At first glance, both the church and the community seemed to be very strong and family friendly. Yet I found myself on a weekly basis trying to help families deal with issues such as sexual and physical abuse, divorce, depression, suicide, money and time management, neglect, pornography, gangs, cults, drugs, alcohol abuse, and so forth. I've seen these same family problems in every church where I've served—no matter the size, denomination or area of the country in which the church was located.

Satan's Strategy

I'm convinced that Satan strategically works to tear apart families so that he can create wounds and scars that will keep people from God and the church for generations. When families go through crises such as the ones listed above, they can easily be torn apart by the waves that crash into them—especially when faith isn't rooted firmly and deeply in the home. When the waves crash down and tear apart the family ship, family members often feel humiliated and embarrassed. They no longer feel worthy to attend church because they don't have it all together. Or they become angry and frustrated, wondering why God would allow this crisis to happen to them.

In either case, Satan accomplishes his objectives of separating people from Christ and causing damage to the effectiveness and witness of the Church. Again, the effects of this damage can last for generations. As Christian Smith, author of *Soul Searching*, notes:

> First, adolescents often associate faith and religion with adults. When adults in teenagers' lives have problems that injure them, religion can become negatively

associated with those problems. Youth can view religion as a source of hypocrisy when adults fail to live up to the standards professed by religion. In this and other ways, religion can become for some youth a symbolic field of resistance or rebellion on which to work out their anger or hurt over the adult problems that bother or injure them. Thus, adult problems imposing on the lives of teens may create subjective dissonances with religion, causing some youth to drift from their congregations and discard their beliefs.[2]

Home Life Affects Church Life

During the past four decades, the American Church has clearly lost a lot of its strength, stability and overall health. In fact, since 1991, the adult population in the United States has grown by 15 percent but the number of adults who don't attend church has nearly doubled, rising from 39 million to 75 million—a 92 percent increase![3]

According to a 2001 study conducted by the Graduate Center of City University of New York, the United States appears to be going through an unprecedented change in religious practices. Large numbers of American adults are disaffiliating themselves from Christianity and from other organized religions. Since World War II, this process had been observed in other countries, including Canada, Australia, New Zealand, the United Kingdom and other European nations. But until recently, affiliation with Christianity had been at a high level—about 87 percent—and stable.

U.S. polling data from the study indicates that 81 percent of American adults identify themselves with a specific religion; 76.5 percent of which identify themselves as Christian (159 million). This is a major slide from the 86.2 percent reported in 1990. Identification with Christianity has suffered a loss of 9.7 percentage points in 11 years—about 0.9 percentage points per year. This decline is identical to that observed in Canada between 1981 and 2001. If this trend continues, by about the year 2042, non-Christians will outnumber the Christians in the United States.[4] Furthermore, a *USA Today*/Gallup Poll conducted in January 2002 shows that almost half of American adults appear to be alienated from organized religion. If current trends continue, most adults won't call themselves religious within a few years.[5]

Not so coincidentally, during the past four decades the American family has lost a lot of its strength, stability and overall health. The high divorce rate that has existed for several generations—along with our nation's consumerism, materialism and ever-increasing pace of life—is taking a toll on families. Families are being pulled apart from a variety of directions. I'm convinced that the Church is in turmoil and crisis today because families are in turmoil and crisis. Until we address the family crisis, we can't have a healthy church.

Peter Benson has also stated, "Religious life in the home is more influential than the church." If this statement is true, we need to be asking ourselves some important questions about what this means. How is religious life in the home "going" today? If the future of the Church depends on the current health and stability of families, what does the current health and stability of families look like?

Search Institute conducted a nationwide survey of more than 11,000 participants from 561 congregations across 6 different denominations. The results were quite revealing (keep in mind that churched youth were surveyed!):

- Twelve percent of youth have a regular dialog with their mother on faith/life issues.

- Five percent of youth have a regular dialog with their father on faith/life issues.
- Nine percent of youth have experienced regular reading of the Bible and devotions in the home.
- Twelve percent of youth have experienced a servanthood event with a parent as an action of faith.[6]

In his research for his book *Transforming Children into Spiritual Champions,* researcher George Barna confirmed these results: "We discovered that in a typical week, fewer than 10 percent of parents who regularly attend church with their kids read the Bible together, pray together (other than at meal times) or participate in an act of service as a family unit. Even fewer families—1 out of every 20—have any type of worship experience together with their kids, other than while they are at church during a typical month."[7]

Based on these findings, we can easily come to the conclusion that religious life in the home is almost nonexistent.

Losing the Home

What difference does it make that religious life in the home is nearly extinct? As pastors and church leaders, we must face the reality that we are losing the primary place of influence for faith development—the home. Mom and Dad have always been the primary nurturers of faith. In *The Family as Forming Center,* Marjorie Thompson writes, "For all their specialized training, church professionals realize that if a child is not receiving basic Christian nurture in the home, even the best teachers and curriculum will have minimal impact. Once-a-week exposure simply cannot compete with daily experience where personal formation is concerned."[8]

My father was a youth and family pastor in the 1960s and 1970s. During these years, the Church saw an explosion in Christian education through Sunday School and youth group ministries. Churches added education wings and youth rooms to their facilities, and these programs brought a lot of excitement to the churches. At the same time, families began to get busier as society moved out of the industrial age and into the technological age. Work schedules increased and more moms began to get jobs outside of the home. When churches began offering ministries for children and teenagers, parents welcomed the opportunity to bring their kids for a time of Christian education and fun. Quite honestly, for many parents this also provided a needed break from their children.

While everyone's intentions were good, what churches failed to realize is that many parents saw these programs as an opportunity to pass on the faith-nurturing responsibilities to the Church. Parents dropped off their kids and said, "Here you go; teach my children faith. I'll be back in an hour to pick them up."

Of course, the Church never intended for these programs to take the place of parents in the faith development of children. However, intentional or not, during the last 40 to 50 years, we've moved away from the home being the primary place where faith is nurtured. As George Barna notes, "A majority of churches are actually guilty of perpetuating an unhealthy and unbiblical process wherein the church usurps the role of the family and creates an unfortunate, sometimes exclusive, dependency upon the church for a child's spiritual nourishment."[9]

Just as parents take their children to a soccer coach for them to learn soccer or to a piano teacher for them to learn piano, they bring their children to the church for them to learn faith. This drop-off approach might—at best—keep kids busy in church for a few years, but it usually doesn't lead to any kind of lasting faith in their adult years. Peter Benson notes, "Teaching values through programs is useful, but it is secondary in impact to how cultures have always passed on the best of human wisdom: through wisdom modeled, articulated, practiced, and discussed by adults with children around them. It is learning through engagement with responsible adults that nurtures value development and requires intergenerational community. Programs are an important reinforcement, but they are not the primary process."[10]

Lasting Impressions

Not only are programs not the primary process for teaching faith and values, but they are also not the biblical model.

Right after Moses called together the Israelites to deliver what we call the Ten Commandments, he described to the people how they were to live as followers of God. These ways would allow them to prosper as families and as a community of believers: "Impress them [the commands of the Bible] on your children. Talk about them when you sit at home and when you walk along the road, when you lie down and when you get up. . . . The Lord commanded us to obey all these decrees and to fear the Lord our God, so that we might always prosper and be kept alive, as is the case today" (Deut. 6:7,24).

Wouldn't you like to know how to live life in a way that you and your church family would always prosper? Moses stated that we can "live long and prosper" by impressing the biblical way of life on our children by living it out at home: "When you sit at home and when you walk along the road, when you lie down [which takes place at home] and when you get up [which also takes place at home]."

Notice that Moses didn't say taking children to Sunday School and dropping them off at the front door was some mystical way for them to learn faith. In fact, after 15 years in ministry, I can tell you that no matter how good a Sunday School or youth program is, if children don't see godly living modeled and hear issues of values and faith discussed in the home, any faith they gain at church probably will not stick when they grow older.

Faith that Doesn't Stick

Eddie was a perfect example of a child whose faith didn't stick. He was involved in every youth program we had. He came to every youth night we held, attended every retreat and summer camp we offered, and became a leader in our youth program. Yet we never saw his parents except when they picked him up or dropped him off at church. At one retreat, when I asked him about his mom and dad, he said, "They don't believe in Jesus, but they think church is a safe place for me to hang out. So that's why they let me stay involved in church."

When Eddie graduated from high school, he didn't have the money to attend college. So he worked. For a while, he stayed around church to help out with the youth program. But gradually, we saw less and less of him. About 18 months after graduating from high school, Eddie was picked up for drunk driving. That was just the beginning of a series of problems Eddie would have.

Today, Eddie hasn't set foot in church for years. It makes me wonder how a leader of a church youth group—someone who clearly demonstrated a strong personal faith in Christ— could abandon his faith and end up in jail just a few years later. I believe the answer is that his faith was never firmly "impressed" on and in him. His faith wasn't grounded at home. In fact, something else was impressed on Eddie: His dad was an alcoholic who began to buy Eddie alcohol after his high school graduation, even though he was underage, and his mom didn't really care if he continued going to church or not. Due to the influence Eddie received in his home, faith looked like a program rather than a lifestyle to him. When the program was done, so was Eddie.

You've probably heard what I'm about to say before. But I hope that if you remember nothing else from this book, you'll remember this: *Faith is not something that can be taught; faith is something that must be caught.*

It's like catching a cold. When my daughter, Malyn, catches a cold at school and brings the virus into our home, Maria and I inevitably also catch the cold! That's how faith works: When faith is in the home, everyone catches it! As pastors and leaders of Christ's church, we should be doing everything we can to get faith talk and living back into the homes and everyday life of the people of our churches. We must reestablish the home as the primary place where faith is nurtured.

Losing the Influencers

Why is reestablishing the home as the main place for faith development so important? The main reason is the influence of Mom and Dad—who are two to three times more influential than any church program.

I remember when I was confronted with this reality. In my early years as a youth and family pastor, I was satisfied if I had a lot of teenagers involved in our youth programs. I thought I was doing my job if I reached teens for Christ, got them involved in church programs and took them on youth trips and to Bible camp. One day, I received a questionnaire to give to the teenagers in my youth group. The survey was titled "The Most Significant Religious Influences."[11] The survey was conducted by the Search Institute to help determine what factors influenced teens in their faith.[12]

Mainline Protestant Youth Most Significant Religious Influences*

MOST SIGNIFICANT RELIGIOUS INFLUENCES	Percent Choosing as One of Top 5							
	GRADE						GENDER	
	7th	8th	9th	10th	11th	12th	M	F
Mother	87	75	77	72	75	75	81	74
Father	64	51	55	49	57	51	61	50
Grandparent	36	28	29	34	27	22	30	29
Another relative	11	12	14	16	12	7	13	12
Siblings	22	14	13	13	15	14	18	14
Friends	22	24	28	25	31	31	22	29
Pastor	60	56	49	45	36	49	57	44
Church camp	23	30	26	25	23	23	20	28
Movie/music star	3	3	4	4	2	2	4	3
Christian Education at my church	23	30	25	25	31	25	26	26
Church school teacher	29	27	17	23	20	23	26	21
Youth Group at my church	25	25	32	33	33	34	30	30
Youth Group Leader at my church	13	11	20	17	17	15	15	16
Youth Group outside my church	3	6	2	3	4	5	4	4
Youth Group Leader outside my church	2	1	1	3	4	4	2	3
The Bible	25	30	27	23	16	26	24	25
Other books I have read	2	3	4	4	3	4	3	4
Prayer of meditation	9	15	15	16	20	18	11	19
School teacher	3	5	2	2	3	6	3	4
Revivals or rallies	3	3	4	4	5	4	3	4
TV or radio evangelist	2	·	1	·	·	·	1	1
Worship services at church	10	10	10	16	14	15	12	13
God in my life	3	3	11	11	13	13	8	13
Work camp	·	1	4	2	5	5	3	3
Mission study tour	0	0	·	0	1	1	·	·
Retreats	7	12	16	20	17	18	11	17
Coach	2	2	3	3	4	4	4	2
Choir or music at church	11	12	8	9	11	6	7	12

*Includes mainline Protestant youth only (CC, ELCA, PCUSA, UCC, UMC) weighted by congregational and denomination size.

I strategically gave the questionnaire to my students after we had been on a youth trip together, hoping to increase my score as their youth pastor. As instructed, I collected the surveys and returned them to the Search Institute. It took months to get the results, but I still remember receiving the envelope stamped with the words, "Survey Results Inside." I was on my way to a youth board meeting and I thought this would be the opportunity of a lifetime. I was certain that the results would show that I, the esteemed youth and family pastor, was the top influencer in the faith journey of our church's youth. I even wondered if these results would strengthen my case for a raise.

At the youth board meeting, I opened the letter and began to read the results: "The most significant religious influence for Christian teens today is . . . Mom." At first I was upset, but then I quickly rationalized that no one can compete with moms. So I moved on: "The second most significant religious influence for Christian teens today is . . . Dad." This one hurt. I had been around most of the dads of the teens in my youth group, and I knew that I spent more time with their kids than they did! How could dads possibly be more influential than I was?

My heart continued to sink as significant religious influence number three was a grandparent, followed by friends and siblings. "Youth group leader at my church" was way down the list. At that point, I accepted the reality that parents are the primary influences in the faith development of children.

In *Soul Searching,* Christian Smith summarizes, "Most teenagers and their parents may not realize it, but a lot of research in the sociology of religion suggests that the most important social influence in shaping young people's religious lives is the religious life modeled and taught to them by their parents."[13]

What Does It All Mean?

The Bible makes clear (and research confirms) that the home is the primary place where faith must be nurtured. Both Scripture and research conclude that parents are the most important influences in passing on faith to children. So these truths beg the question: *Why do we focus almost all of our time, energy and resources on what takes place at church?*

In other words, if religious life in the home influences the faith of children more than what happens at church, and if parents are two to three times more influential than any church program, shouldn't we be investing the majority of our time and resources on equipping the home to be the primary place for nurturing faith?

When I was confronted with this information and this reality, I had a choice to make. I could continue leading and offering programs at church that would keep me and the people who attended our church busy, or I could reexamine everything our church did through a set of lenses that focused on how this could be bridged to the home. In other words, I had to stop myself and simply ask, "What are we accomplishing?"

What Are We Accomplishing at Church?

Remember when a week of Bible camp meant living in a tent, cooking over a fire with a few other kids your age, and going to an evening campfire led by a couple of guitar players? Ah, life was simple then! If you went to a week of Bible camp today, you would find yourself surrounded by hundreds of kids. Your day would be filled with swimming pools, rock climbing, wake boarding, Christian bands, videos, incredible motivational speakers, dining centers and worship spaces with all the technological bells and whistles—maybe even a laser light show!

Even programs in churches, such as Vacation Bible School and Sunday School curriculum, have become more and more creative and engaging. Each year, Bible study resources include more and more options through DVD and Internet enhancements. So over the past 40 years, we've seen the best programs for children, youth and adults ever created in the history of the Church. Yet at the end of the day, if you honestly evaluated the condition of families, would you say they are any better than they were 40 years ago? If you asked some of the senior adults in your church if families are better or worse off today when it comes to talking about and living out their faith in their homes, what kind of answers would you expect?

Although this is hard to admit, we need to be honest. The time, resources and energy we've devoted to programs over the past 40 years hasn't instilled faith-at-home living. Unfortunately, this focus might have even caused some of the problems we face today.

Recently, I spent two weeks speaking in Australia, a country where the evangelical church is considered by many to be 20 to 30 years behind the American evangelical church. I found myself continually saying, "Learn from us. Don't do what we've done." As I spoke, I realized even more acutely that many of our church programs enable a drop-off mentality and that as a result we've helped create a home environment without faith at its center. We have a lot of people coming to our programs at church, but they're no longer living out their faith at home.

In *Rock-Solid Kids,* Larry Fowler shares an experience he had in Kazakhstan that emphasizes what has been lost in many American churches and families:

> The gathering lasted three hours. Three sermons. Men sat on one side of the church, women on the other. All the children were seated in the balcony. Latecomers

stood in the aisle the entire time. Communion was observed with a common cup with real wine. All the music sounded mournful. No smiles. The call to repentance took 45 minutes.

For a Westerner with experience only in western evangelical churches, the Russian church service in Kazakhstan was certainly eye opening.

As a special guest and one of the preachers, I sat on the stage behind the pulpit, facing the audience. I especially noticed the children in the balcony—they were all ages, from four or five years old up through the teens. Their parents weren't with them; only a few adults were scattered among the children. They amazed me—they sat still for the whole three hours! I thought of what American children would do, and I wondered how the Russians did it.

But why did the children attend the entire service? Later, I asked my Russian hosts, "Don't you have a Sunday School for the children?" Their blank look revealed that they didn't understand my concern. 'The parents teach them' was their simple explanation.

I thought this answer was weird. They didn't seem to want a children's Sunday school. They didn't seem to *need* a children's Sunday school. And my team and I were there to present Awana, a midweek children's ministry, to them? How could we get them to start Awana when they didn't even see the need for a Sunday school?

That church, and others in Kazakhstan, have now used the Awana club ministry for 10 years. But they have used it to evangelize the unsaved, not to disciple their own children. And if you ask them why, they will tell you that they don't need it, that the parents teach the children.

Strange, huh? Or is it?[14]

What I'm *Not* Saying

Before you read on, I need you to know that I do not believe we need to throw out the baby with the bathwater and eliminate or completely change worship, Sunday School, men's and women's ministry, Vacation Bible School, youth ministry, camps, retreats, and so on. I've personally experienced just how effective and critical these programs can be when it comes to passing on faith to children, youth and adults. Without them, we would certainly be in even bigger trouble. However, I do believe that we need to take a serious look at these ministries through a set of lenses that focus on equipping the home to be the primary place where faith is nurtured.

Think about this for a moment. No matter how effective our ministries and programs are, Mom and Dad remain two to three times more influential than anything that takes place in our churches! It seems clear that we should then devote some considerable time, effort and resources to what's most effective and God-ordained. Unfortunately, what we often tend to do instead is conclude, "If I just had a better children's or youth program, or if I just had a better children's or youth pastor, our ministry would be more effective."

We need to candidly examine ourselves and realize the erroneous thinking behind these kinds of statements. I've had the opportunity to travel across the country and speak to the leaders of some of the largest and fastest-growing churches in the nation. Even the biggest and strongest churches—those with the best programs and most talented and dynamic leaders—face the same faith at home difficulties. One youth pastor recently told me, "After all these years of trying every different method, program and approach, I've finally come to the realization that our effectiveness is only as good as what happens in the home."

As pastors and church leaders, it's time for us to face the truth: The best personnel for teaching our children and youth about matters of faith are *parents,* and the best programs to teach those matters of faith are the ones that take place in the home. Until we face this fact, we'll continue to chase our tails trying to find the next best program or the next best leader. Again, Larry Fowler summarizes this well:

> If we are to develop a biblically based children's ministry, the first question we should ask is, "Whose job is it?" Who should own the ministry? Who is responsible to train the children? The Bible is clear. *Parents.* Not children's workers in the church. *Parents.* Not children's organizations or children's publishers. *Parents.* Not Christian schools. *Parents.*[15]

Problems We All Face

I hope that you're beginning to realize the playing field has been leveled. Regardless of the size of church we serve, when it comes to equipping people to apply faith and biblical living to their everyday lives at home, we all face the same difficult realities. To confirm this, let's look at some common problems confronting us.

Problem 1: Declining Engagement

One common symptom of a program-driven faith is that as a person's age increases, his or her attendance and participation decline. Dawson McAlister, a national youth ministry specialist, says, "Ninety percent of kids active in high school youth groups do not go to church by the time they are sophomores in college. One third will never return."[16]

In the typical American program-driven church, it's considered normal to see a decline in participation as children grow older. It's not unusual for a church to have 40 students per class when the children are between the ages 5 to 10 but then see the numbers decline to 20 students per class when they reach ages 11 to 15 and then only 10 students per class when they reach ages 16 to 18.

We rationalize this decline with statements such as, "Kids today are so busy that they just don't have time for church." My response to that is simply, "You're probably right. They don't have time for another program. But faith isn't supposed to be about a program. It's supposed to be about a relationship, and kids will make time for relationships that matter to them."

Maria and I have the privilege of being in a small group with four other families. Each has made a commitment to bringing Christ and Christlike living into the center of their homes. Together, we have 10 adults and 12 kids ranging in ages from 8 to 16. I've noticed that as our children grow older, none of them are becoming any less involved in church. If anything, they're becoming more involved and more committed—to the point that they sometimes drag us to church events! I believe that the teenagers have seen their parents actively involved in a personal relationship with Jesus Christ and that this has influenced the decisions they have made and the activities in which they have become involved. As a result, these teenagers are following in their parents' footsteps of faith.

Why don't some teenagers stay engaged in their faith? Because for many, faith was really nothing more than a program they attended. As they got older and wiser, they started to see faith as hypocritical, because their parents acted one way at church and a completely different way at home. When these teenagers became young adults, they concluded, "If that's what Christianity is about, I don't want anything to do with it."

If we want our children to have a faith that influences the way they live and the critical life decisions they make, we need to be modeling faith through a personal relationship with Jesus Christ in our homes. We shouldn't simply write off declining attendance and participation as normal or because kids today are so busy. It's not normal! It's a symptom of the problem we face, and it needs to be addressed.

Problem 2: Drop-off Mentality

As I mentioned earlier, for many families today, church is sometimes no more than a safe drop-off center for kids. Not long ago, Maria was reading a magazine article as she ran on the treadmill. The article gave readers ideas about how they could add 30 minutes to their day. The last suggestion almost made her fall off the treadmill. One woman proudly stated that she had found a way to get two hours more out of her week by dropping her kids off at church and running errands while they were in Sunday School! Why not? After all, church is a place that will teach children good morals, keep them out of trouble and surround them with other good kids their age.

At Ventura Missionary Church, where I serve as pastor, we have a K to 8 school. Some 40 percent of the students who attend our school come from unchurched families. Most of these parents are hardworking people who make a significant financial sacrifice to enroll their children in our private school. Each weekday morning, these parents pull into our parking lot and drop off their children with the expectation that we will teach them good morals and solid faith. Yet when we urge parents to be a part of teaching these same morals and faith with their children at home, they often dig in their heels and say, "That's what we pay you to do."

Of course, it's easy to see how this happens in a private-school situation. But if you don't think it also happens in your children's and youth programs, you simply have blinders on.

Many of the people who enroll their children and youth in church programs do so with the same "drop-off" expectations. I don't think this was God's intention when He created the Church.

I agree with George Barna when he states, "The local church should be an intimate and valuable partner in the effort to raise the coming generation of Christ's followers and church leaders, but it is the parents whom God will hold primarily accountable for the spiritual maturation of their children."[17] When I lead a new-member class at our church, I'm pretty blunt in stating that if people are looking for a church where they can drop off their children and expect us to teach them faith, then we're not the right church for them. Of course, I also add that we would gladly come alongside them and partner with them to bring Christ and Christlike living into the center of their homes.

Problem 3: Loss of Standing

Many families today don't recognize the Church as a resource that can help them with their family relationships. They will quickly turn to TV and radio shrinks, the Internet, counseling and even medication to help them as a family, but the Church isn't even a blip on their radar.

One time, I worked with a family who had been through an ugly divorce. The parents battled almost every situation through lawsuits and court cases. They tried counseling but quit out of frustration. As is often the case, the children found themselves continually in the middle of their parents' warfare.

I became involved in the situation because the teenage daughter, Abby, started attending our youth worship service through the invitation of a school friend. Eventually, Abby joined a small group and began to open up. Things hit rock bottom one Friday night when she came to church and asked to meet with me. She informed me that her mom was home drunk because she had just had another fight with her ex-husband. Abby didn't know what to do, so we called her mom and got permission for her to stay at her friend's house that night.

The next day, I went over to meet with Abby's mom. When I arrived, I was greeted rather abruptly. "Who are you and what do you want?" she said.

"My name is Pastor Mark," I said as politely as I could. "Abby is part of our youth group, and I was wondering if we could talk for a minute."

I could tell by her reaction that she was somewhat surprised and a bit ashamed. "I'm sorry," she responded more softly, "I thought you were a door-to-door salesman." She invited me in, and after a few minutes I informed her that Abby had told me about the ugly divorce and the drinking problem she had. I asked if there was anything I could do to help.

The look of brokenness in her eyes said it all as she struggled to reply. I looked her in the eyes and said softly, "Ma'am, I'm not here to judge you or to preach to you. I just want you to know that you, your children and even your ex-husband matter to God. We would welcome the opportunity to show you how Christ wants to help you and your family."

The woman broke into tears, and after a few moments she replied, "I used to go to church before all this happened. But after all of this mess, I thought church was only for families who had it all together and that I was no longer welcome."

Over the course of the next two years, we were able to come alongside this family and see God work many miracles. Abby now attends a Christian college and is studying to be a youth pastor. Her mom made a complete turnaround and is now remarried to a wonderful Christian man.

While Abby's story is great news, the point I'm trying to make is that the Church needs to get back on the radar for families. If it hadn't been for Abby, her mom probably would never have set foot in a church during her time of crisis and need.

Whether she was right or wrong, she had pegged the Church as a place only for families that are healthy and put together. The Church needs to break that stereotype and put out a welcome mat that reads, "*All* families are welcome here"!

Problem 4: Ill-equipped Parents

A while back, I was speaking to a group of parents and teenagers. I began my talk by asking a series of questions.

"Raise your hand if you think you could name one of the 12 disciples." Nearly every hand in the room went up.

"Raise your hand if you could name a living disciple today." Just a few hands went up.

"Raise your hand if you believe in Jesus Christ as your Lord and Savior." Again, every hand went up.

I then told the teenagers and parents to look at each other, and made the following statement: "Realize that the person you're looking at—who stated he or she believes in Jesus Christ as Lord and Savior—is a disciple of Jesus Christ." The crowd began to murmur a little. From the front row, one boy pointed his finger at his dad and loudly proclaimed, "No way—not *him*!" The boy wanted to go on to tell all the ways his father wasn't a disciple of Christ! Obviously, this wasn't the point of the exercise, but it did make for a powerful illustration. Our children are watching us to see if our behaviors reflect the faith we proclaim.

Many parents today would rather pass instilling their children's faith on to the "professionals" at church instead of tackling this responsibility themselves. Because they often didn't experience what it was like to have Christ as a part of the home they grew up in, they don't have a model to follow. As each generation becomes less and less involved in the Christian Church—and, as a result, with faith at home—more and more parents are now two to three generations removed from the last generation that remembers having faith talk, Bible reading, devotions and prayer in the home.

Talk to the parents in your church and you'll find that they have a desire to bring "spirituality," as they might call it, into the home. But they have absolutely no idea how to do this, because they never experienced these matters of faith in their home when they were growing up. Even the strongest families in your church might surprise you with their lack of ability to talk with their children about faith or even a willingness to pray together as a family.

The Thompson family in my church was a perfect example of this. One day, Alan Thompson, an active member of our congregation, called my office. While he often chatted with me at church, he rarely called. I immediately presumed something was wrong. He stammered a bit, searching for the right words and then said, "I'm having troubles with my 15-year-old, Andrea."

"What do you mean by 'troubles'?" I asked.

"We're not communicating real well, and it seems like we're always on opposite ends of every situation. I'd like to talk with you to see if there is anything I can do so that we're not always fighting."

Realizing that he needed more than a quick answer over the phone, I decided to go visit the family at their home. Alan, his wife and two children lived in a beautiful home. By the world's standards, they appeared to have everything together. Alan was involved in a variety of committees at church, and his wife helped out with Sunday School. Andrea was actively involved in the youth ministry and also helped teach Sunday School.

When I arrived, Alan invited me in and we sat down to talk in the living room. For the first 30 minutes, he shared story after story with me of how disrespectful Andrea had become. "She doesn't listen to me anymore," he exclaimed. "Whenever I establish a rule or guideline, she always seems to push just beyond the limit. That forces me to have to do something about it. I'm also concerned about the friends she's hanging out with. I'm wondering if I need to limit how much time she can spend with them."

As Alan continued ticking off his concerns, I thought to myself, *What am I going to say? I don't have a teenager and I've never had to face this myself.* When he had finally exhausted himself of stories, he turned to me and said, "What am I supposed to do?"

Not wanting to let on that I actually felt ill-equipped to handle his family's situation, I did what I always try to do when I get in over my head: I turned to God for help. Then I sat back in the chair, turned to him and said, "Have you prayed with Andrea about this?"

This didn't seem like an outrageous question to me. I had seen Alan lead prayer many times at committee meetings, and his daughter led prayer in Sunday School every week. Yet the look in his eyes told me all I needed to know.

During the first 15 years of Andrea's life, Alan had been actively involved in taking her to daycare, soccer practice, piano lessons and even church. But he had never prayed with her. The idea of praying with his daughter for the first time as a teenager now seemed utterly beyond the scope of reason.

Many parents share this feeling that they are ill equipped to lead their children in the faith. I once co-led a workshop with David Anderson called "Nurturing Faith of Teenagers." I set the stage by helping parents list and outline the characteristics and issues of teenagers today. Dr. Anderson then took it a step further by asking the parents, "How many of you here today wish your teenager had a stronger faith?" Every hand in the room went up. He then made a comment that I'll never forget "While it's good that we all desire our teenagers have a stronger faith, the reality is that what we see in our teenagers' faith is simply a mirror image of our faith. So the issue is not their faith, but our faith."

As we noted earlier, Scripture clearly states that parents have both the responsibility and honor to pass on the faith to their children (see Deut. 6). Martin Luther put it this way: "Most certainly father and mother are apostles, bishops, and priests to their children, for it is they who make them acquainted with the gospel."[18] Think about that for a minute. Imagine if every parent in your church thought of themselves as a bishop, apostle and priest to their children. That's what I call a "home as church too" vision! However, for that vision to become a reality, we need to train and equip parents to be the bishops, apostles and priests in their own homes.

Problem 5: Competition

Another problem that we must face isn't actually a problem with the Church, but it's still a problem. It's the reality that families today have more things competing for their time than ever before. Whether or not we want to admit it, the Church is in competition with the world.

Jack Eggar, president and CEO of Awana Clubs International, once said, "There has never been a time in history when the children of the world have been more spiritually at risk than they are today. A plethora of competing worldviews and warped values flow freely throughout society—directly into the minds of children, where they stay for a lifetime."[19]

Just a few decades ago, the Church played a much more significant role in the lives of families. It wasn't unusual to see businesses closed on Sundays, and public schools wouldn't give homework on Wednesdays because that evening was "church night." Families were committed to being at church whenever the doors were open. And families frequently came together with other like-minded families who attended church for fellowship, fun and even vacation!

Recently, I had a chance to experience a blast from the past when I was asked to speak at Brown City Family Camp, one of the nation's largest family camps. This family camp, which is located on a 12-acre piece of property in northern Michigan, has been running for more than 75 years. The camp only opens for two weeks of family camp each year, and it draws more than 2,000 people from all over Michigan. These families spend an intense week eating together, worshiping together, singing together, playing together and shutting off all the noise from the outside world (that's right—no TVs, computers or cell phones) just to be with God and each other. The camp draws families ranging from those with newborns to those with members who are more than 90 years old. It is truly an intergenerational gathering.

As I walked around and talked with people, the one comment I heard repeatedly was simply, "We wouldn't miss this family camp for anything. This is the best thing our family does every year." Today, however, hardly anyone would think of spending such an intense week as a family with other Christian families. Few people even recognize the concept of a "church night." Sunday morning is business as usual. If anything, the Church now competes with sports leagues and other extracurricular activities that vie for the family's time—even on Sunday mornings.

I believe that Satan knows the Christian Church is one of the most valuable resources families need to succeed. So he will do everything he can to keep people from getting connected to an intentional Christian community. One of his tools is to get families so busy that they don't have time for church. And, quite simply, when families don't have time for church, they can't establish a lasting partnership with it.

Shortly after Malyn was born, Maria and I joined a small group at our church with three other couples who all had children less than six months old. At the time, we wondered if this would be worth the time and effort. At first, none of the parents were sure if it would work, but we continued to meet. Over time, the relationships grew and the small group became a place where we could share the highs and lows of trying to be a family in a crazy world.

Eleven years have passed, and many more children have come into the picture. We've laughed together and cried together.

We've been through job losses, cancer diagnosis and treatment, family crises, depression and relocation. We've learned how to parent together and how to bring God into the center of our homes.

When we started this home group, we had no idea what we were doing. But now we wouldn't know how to do life without each other. Today, this group is as important to us as family—so important that we still get together two or three times a year, even though we are separated by more than 2,000 miles.

God doesn't want us to go through life alone. His Word says, "Let us not give up meeting together, as some are in the habit of doing, but let us encourage one another" (Heb. 10:25).

So, Just What Are We Accomplishing?

While no one intended church programs to cause or enable families to disengage from living out their faith in the home, the fact remains that faithful Christlike living isn't occurring in homes today. We must face the problems that this has created.

Obviously, we can't go back in time and change our reality. Instead, we must face what has taken place and begin the work of making changes that will have an impact on our future. Religious life in the home is more influential than the Church. Mom and Dad are more influential than any church program. So as church leaders, we should be focusing on the home as the primary place where faith is nurtured.

I once read a *USA Today* article that described the different forms of family that exist in our culture today. Do you know how many forms of family this article identified? Twenty-eight! While this number might seem overwhelming, I see it as good news, because no matter how many forms of families we have in our congregations, they all have the same need—Jesus Christ in the center of the home!

As pastors and church leaders, we must take a look at what our role is going to be in bringing Christ and Christlike living back into the center of every home—whether that home is an intact nuclear family, a single-person household, a grandparent living in a nursing home, or a remarried couple with four children.

If you're up to the challenge for your church, let's next look at where we need to be personally to lead this change.

Ponder, Pray and Discuss

1. Reflect on the statement, "As the family goes, so goes the future of the Church." Do you agree or disagree? Why?

2. Have you ever surveyed the teenagers in your church to see what percentage of them:

   • Pray in the home?
   • Read the Bible with their parents at home?
   • Have ever performed a service project as a family?
   • Engage in some sort of faith talk with their mom at least once per month?
   • Engage in some sort of faith talk with their dad at least once per month?

   What do you think the teenagers in your church would say if you asked them these questions? Reflect on your answer.

3. How does the statistical information regarding faith at home affect you? Do you find it challenging? Or do you think it is simply something you should pass on to the leaders of your children's and youth ministries?

CHAPTER 2 SUMMARY:

- The competition for top priority in your ministry.

- The need to gain a passion for making faith at home ministry your top priority.

- Your legacy: reestablishing home as the primary place where faith is nurtured.

- Parents today are searching for a better way to "do family."

- God desires that families not just survive but also thrive.

- Become a pastor whose heart bleeds for families.

- The "God Things" that gave me a passion, a vision and a model for the faith at home movement.

- The struggle with making faith a priority in your own home.

- Bringing Christ back into the center of the home is about *you* and *your* passion and commitment.

- The blessings your family will enjoy when you bring Christ back into the center of your home.

- The blessings your church will enjoy when members bring Christ back to the center of their homes.

Do We Care?

I have never seen parents more hungry for help than they are now.
They want to spend more time with their children. They feel acutely
the need to be better equipped as parents.[1]
Mark DeVries

I'll always remember the day I was talking with some fellow pastors in our community about the condition of families. I invited them to participate in a meeting that our church was hosting to discuss how local churches and pastors could work together to reclaim homes and families for Christ.

As I extended this invitation, the blank stares I received told me everything I needed to know. "That's not my thing," one pastor said to me. "It's simply not something I have any interest in attending."

This kind of reaction isn't limited to the pastors in my community. A few years ago, George Barna conducted a series of daylong seminars across the country that covered four major issues facing the Church. One of the four sessions focused on the importance of children and family ministry. George had previously conducted similar one-day seminars on different topics, but with this series, something happened that he had never seen before. Instead of simply registering for the all-day seminar, numerous pastors called his office and said, "I'm planning to come to your seminar, but could you tell me when the session on children and family ministry will take place? I don't plan to go to that part of the seminar. In fact, I would like to send my children's pastor to that session."

When it comes to the issue of equipping families to apply faith or biblical living in their everyday lives at home, my heart breaks every time I hear a pastor say, "That's not my thing" or "That's for the children's pastor." I simply can't understand why, as pastors and leaders, we wouldn't want to make building faith at home a top priority in our churches.

I'll admit that until I became a senior pastor, I had no idea how many voices would be calling for me to make various ministries and programs a top priority in the church. The latest prayer magazine arrives and makes a compelling argument that we need to be a church fully committed to prayer. Then a worship magazine comes along stating the importance of making worship top priority. Then an email alerts me to the latest stewardship seminar we need to host because stewardship is the key to the blessings that God wants to pour out in our church. Then I receive a full-color brochure about a missional-living conference urging us to get more engaged in our community. I place that on my desk next to the Purpose Driven Life conference and the small-groups conference that I should be attending. Oh, and global missions Sunday is coming up, and we need to be a church that goes out into all nations to reach people for Christ!

Am I the only one who's overwhelmed and confused?

Where's Your Heart?

I'm guessing that these and other tensions and tugs also demand your time, attention and resources. Yet somehow, here you are reading this book. That means you must have some interest and passion for seeing Christ and Christlike living in the center of every home. With that in mind, how do you feel when you read the following statements from George Barna's research:

- A large majority of believers rely on their church, rather than on their families, to train their children to become spiritually mature.

- In an average month, fewer than 1 out of every 10 churched families worship together outside of a church service. Just as few pray together, other than at mealtimes, and the same minimal numbers study the Bible together at home or work together to address the needs of the disadvantaged people in their community.

- Apart from church-based programs, the typical Christian family spends less than 3 hours per month in endeavors designed to jointly develop or apply their faith.

- Most Christian parents do not believe they are doing a good job at facilitating the spiritual development of their children.[2]

How do these statements make you feel? How do they affect your approach to ministry? As Satan intentionally and methodically takes Christ and Christlike living out of homes, my question to you as a fellow pastor and leader in God's church is simply, "Do you care?"

Of Course You Care!

Please hear me when I say that I know you care. You wouldn't be in ministry unless you cared about Christ, His Church and His people. I know that lost people matter to you, because they matter to Christ. You wouldn't put yourself on the front lines of ministry day after day if you didn't care.

However, I'm asking you to prayerfully consider the fact that in the pursuit of growing our churches, we might have lost sight of what's happening in our homes. Perhaps we need to care a little less about the programs people try to pressure us into making the top priority in our churches so that we can care more about what's happening in the homes and families of the people in our churches. Of all the things you can do as a leader in Christ's church, there is nothing more important than helping to bring Christ and Christlike living into the center of every home.

As a pastor, what do you want your legacy to be? What does success look like to you? Will it just be building a large congregation and a big and beautiful facility? Or will it focus on reestablishing the homes in your community as the primary place where the nurturing of faith takes place?

Here's Your Chance

I love the Church, and I believe God is calling the Church to rise up and address the area that Satan is attacking the most—our families. Through the years, my experience tells me that parents today want to have a better family than the one in which they grew up. They're searching for a better way to "do family." As youth and family pastor Mark DeVries writes, "In my fifteen years of youth ministry, I have never seen parents more hungry for help than they are now. They want to spend more time with their children. They feel acutely the need to be better equipped as parents."[3] Well, here's your chance as a pastor to help equip the parents in your church!

I firmly believe that the Christian church can offer what every family needs to succeed: a personal, growing relationship with Jesus Christ, who knocks at the door of their home and says, "Let Me in, and I'll help your family enjoy long life!" Now is the time for churches to come alongside families and equip them to bring Christ into the center of their homes. This could be our finest hour as the Church! As a pastor I served with once said to me, "The role of the Church isn't to make sure that, as you look down on this community, you can see the light shining bright from our facility. Rather, the role of the Church is to make sure the light shines in each and every home, lighting the community for the world to see!"

God Wants Families to Thrive!

The crisis that families face today isn't just an American problem. It's something pastors and leaders from all over the world must address. When my first book, *Faith Begins at Home*, was taken to a Christian publishing book fair in Germany, it was the most-requested book for translation into German. This was completely unexpected, because I was an unknown author. But I believe this happened because God is beginning to lead a movement to reclaim and reestablish families through His Church. And that's exciting!

Many parents today are searching for help. They want to succeed! They surf the Internet, watch *Oprah* and *Dr. Phil* and buy every self-help book that comes out in an effort to keep their families together for another day. Yet families seem to be hanging on by a thread. In our desperate search for answers, I wonder if we realize that God is there for families. In fact, He desires that families not just survive but also thrive!

The rest of this chapter might seem very personal to you. It is. I want to tell you my own story so that you can more fully understand for yourself how God is at work in leading this movement. I want to share with you some of the things God has done in my life to grow within me the faith at home passion and commitment that now drives me.

The "God Things" in My Life

I didn't always have the passion for building faith at home that I have today. To be honest, I spent a good part of my life without this issue even on my radar. All of this—the passion I have, the vision, the model and the movement for families—is about the Lord, not me. I don't deserve any of the credit. He deserves it all!

At a conference I spoke at recently, I was introduced as "a pastor whose heart bleeds for families." As you read on, you'll see that a lot of "God things" had to take place in my life for this statement to be true. Perhaps God is calling you to be a part of the faith at home movement. If our churches are going to change, the change must begin with us as pastors and leaders. We must be personally convicted and passionate about this, or nothing will change.

So what about you? Does your heart bleed for this?

God Thing 1: Bible Camp Living

Growing up as the son of a Bible camp director provided a unique—some of my friends would say warped—view on how to live for Christ. My family lived at the Bible camp, which meant that I had a 500-acre backyard with hiking trails, horseback-riding trails, soccer fields, softball diamonds, a lake for swimming, and campfires. If I didn't like my friends one week, I knew I would get 100 new ones the next week! My dad served as the executive director, and my mom worked in the office, helped in the kitchen and pretty much served as camp mom to the summer staff. My two older sisters also worked at the camp. Because they were 8 and 10 years older than I, they served as great role models for me.

Most people leave the real world for a spiritual refilling week-end or week at a camp or retreat. Once there, they tune out and leave behind the noise of the outside world and just spend time with God in His creation. At camp, everything focuses on Jesus—from the first thing you do in the morning until the last thing you do at night. But after a weekend or a week, you have to return home and go back to the daily grind.

For me, however, camp living was our real world. This meant that my family's lifestyle at home was pretty much 24/7 living for Christ. We prayed together as a family, went to worship and campfires together, sang Christian songs together, read the Bible together, served together and celebrated all the Christian holidays together. At camp, I saw what life was like when a person lived it completely for Christ. In contrast, church seemed boring to me. So, from a young age, I determined that I would be a camp director like my dad. I certainly didn't want to be a pastor!

During my four years at a Christian college, I worked at a different Bible camp each summer so that I could gain as much experience as possible. After graduation, I began my working career as the full-time program director for a Bible camp in Iowa. I was in my glory, as the camp provided an intentional Christian community where more than 3,000 people each year came for spiritual refueling.

Yet one thing disturbed me. Each week, we saw hundreds of kids get excited and passionate about their relationship with Jesus Christ. As they left camp, you could see the fire they had gained for living for Christ. But during the non-summer months when I preached in some of the congregations these campers came from, I could quickly see that the fire was no longer there. From my limited perspective, I realized that camp fired up kids for Christ while church seemingly served as a great fire extinguisher.

Although this bothered me, I wasn't too concerned because I was planning to always be a Bible camp director. So I didn't have to worry about the Church. At least, that's what I thought.

God Thing 2: Out of Camping Ministry and into the Church
During my fifth summer at this Bible camp, Maria and I went to a wedding in Minneapolis. Throughout the weekend, God seemed to be working in my heart with a new calling. On the drive back to Iowa, I suddenly asked Maria, "What would you think if we left camping ministry and pursued a calling to serve as a youth pastor in a church?"

I'll never forget her response—after the initial shock wore off: "You, Mr. Camp, the person who thinks camp is cool and church is boring, wants to leave camping to serve in a church?" As hard as it was for Maria to believe, it was equally terrifying for me. I had absolutely no congregational ministry experience! I didn't think any congregation would actually call a camp guy to serve their church, so I thought I was safe. Yet God guided us, and one church in a Minneapolis suburb patiently and persistently pursued me to come and serve as their associate minister overseeing youth and family ministry.

It didn't take long for me to realize the front-line nature of congregational ministry. I was constantly bombarded with the hurts and brokenness that occur in families. I began to see and experience firsthand what was happening in the Church. I observed how Satan strategically and methodically tears apart families, creating the pain, confusion and bitterness that turn family members away from God and each other.

Week after week, month after month, and year after year as I worked with people, God began to open my eyes. Prior to this experience, I often blamed the Church for putting out the fires for faithful living that God ignited at camp. But now I was confronted with the truth that the Church wasn't serving as the fire extinguisher—at least not directly.

In many ways, the Church did the same things we did at camp. Yet something was putting out those fires, and now I could see where the fire extinguisher was. It was the home!

Christ and Christlike living clearly weren't happening in people's homes. For the first time, I understood that the type of home life I experienced growing up at camp was radically different than the life that existed in the majority of the families in our church. At this point, God began to break my heart and convict me that we had to do something to rescue families.

God Thing 3: A Mentor and a Child

I could now see the problem, but I didn't have a clue about a solution. At this point, God brought an important person into my life. His name was Dr. Dick Hardel. I had met Dick when I was in camping ministry, where he had spoken a few times at our youth retreats. At the time, he was an assistant to the bishop for the Nebraska synod of the Evangelical Lutheran Church in America. Each time he came to speak, it felt as if I had known him for a long time.

About the same time I accepted the call to leave camping ministry and come to the Minneapolis area, Dick had accepted a position as the director of the Youth and Family Institute in Minneapolis. When we ran into each other at a pastors' conference, we were like two long lost friends who had been separated for years.

Dick had been a successful pastor for years, and he had always made faith at home a top priority in his ministry. Now he was bringing that passion to the Youth and Family Institute, where he could help congregations across the country partner with homes to pass on faith. Between the Institute's research and Dick's incredibly deep knowledge of Scripture and his contagious passion, I became compelled to put faith at home on my radar as a pastor.

As a result of our friendship, Dick and I began working together on ways we could bring Christ and Christlike living back into the home through existing church programs like

Sunday School, youth groups and other ministries. Essentially, he was the "big idea" guy, while I served as the "practitioner." For the next 12 years, I had the privilege of serving in 3 congregations of different sizes (400, 1,200 and 2,500 worshipers). During those years, God began to develop a vision and a continually evolving model for a faith at home ministry that would transform the lives of families.

About the same time, God made the idea of family ministry even more personal for me. On October 31, 1995, Maria and I found ourselves in a birthing room at North Memorial Hospital in Minneapolis. We had been married for five years at the time, but we now stood at the brink of becoming parents for the first time. For three hours, I steadfastly stood by Maria's side, serving as her focal point as she went through contraction after contraction. Then the incredible moment of truth arrived! Our daughter, Malyn, came into the world. What an amazing sight to see!

Immediately, the nurses whisked her away to the other side of the room to clean and measure her. Malyn was crying loudly, but Maria was also groaning from the pain of delivering her first child. To this day, I remember standing halfway between them wondering, *Which way do I go? Do I go to the side of my wife, who has just gone through one of the most exhausting and painful experiences of her life? Or do I go to the side of my precious little girl who is crying for the first time?*

Then the voice of God spoke to me—which, oddly, sounded a lot like Maria—and commanded, "Go make sure Malyn is okay." My daughter had been in the world for just 60 seconds, and as a parent I already needed help!

I'll never forget the first time I held this precious gift from God in my arms. I remember thinking, *Now what do I do?* I desperately wanted Malyn to know the love of Christ and to grow to love Jesus with all her heart, soul and strength. Yet we weren't living at a Bible camp, so we didn't have that environment to help us. I needed help, and I knew it! My work as a youth and family ministry pastor suddenly became intensely personal. It was as much for me as it was for anyone in the congregations I would serve.

God Thing 4: A Playground

Back in my college years, one of my best friends was a guy named Darel. He and I enjoyed playing basketball, golf, cards and pretty much anything competitive. We lived on the edge a bit, yet we always looked out for each other. After graduation, Darel met a young woman named Laura who quickly took hold of his heart. A couple of years later, he called and said that he and Laura were getting married, and he wanted me to help with the wedding.

Laura's dad, Steve, was the senior pastor of a fairly large church in Sioux City, Iowa. While he wanted to give the message for the wedding, he also wanted to just be the bride's dad for the rest of the service. I gladly agreed to take part, and on the weekend of the wedding, I had an opportunity to meet Steve as we worked through the ceremony. Steve was a great guy, and we had a lot of fun doing the service together. Yet little did I know that God had another purpose in mind.

About five years later, Steve took a call to serve as senior pastor of Calvary Lutheran Church in Golden Valley, Minnesota—one of the largest Lutheran churches in the nation. Steve's first task was to put together a new team of pastors to lead the ministry forward. One of the key positions was a pastor who would take charge of the entire children, youth and family ministry program at the church. This position meant overseeing a full-time staff of 12, a budget of nearly one million dollars, and programs that served approximately 1,500 children and youth.

Because of our previous encounter at Darel and Laura's wedding, Steve knew that I was a youth and family pastor. When he called and asked if I would consider interviewing for the position, I was both surprised and excited. Calvary was one of the leading congregations in youth and family ministry, and the opportunity to serve in a church of this size and with the resources they had was truly a dream opportunity. Following a series of interviews, Calvary offered me the opportunity to come and join their team. For five years, I was blessed to serve as their youth and family pastor.

Calvary was the greatest playground in the world for me. I had the opportunity to be creative and work with some of the most innovative leaders in youth and family ministry. Many years before I arrived, the church had made a commitment to being a faith at home congregation. While serving there, I was blessed to see how God could positively influence and change families when a church stuck with this commitment over an extended period of time.

Everything we did at Calvary with children, youth and families we did from the perspective of how it would affect the home. We watched as God truly transformed families. In addition, we began to have the opportunity to share our model with other congregations across the country. George Barna even contacted us and profiled us as an effective church in his book *Transforming Children into Spiritual Champions*.

God began to grow in me a desire to see other churches and church leaders infected with the passion to make faith at home a priority in their ministries. Now that I was in a church that was fully devoted to this model, I wanted other churches to experience the fruit that we were seeing. Soon, a conceptual model for a comprehensive and integrated faith at home ministry was birthed.

Let me be clear: We didn't create a program. Rather, we created a conceptual model for how the Church needs to "do church" in order to reestablish the home as the primary place where faith can be nurtured. God was developing in me and in the churches I had the opportunity to work with a passion to look at everything we did through a set of lenses that focused on how everything that took place at church affected and equipped the home.

God Thing 5: A Senior Pastor's Perspective

Maria and I both thought I would serve at Calvary forever, but God wasn't done yet. He had even more that He wanted to do in and through us. I'll never forget the day that Pastor Steve gently asked if I had ever considered becoming a senior pastor. He wasn't trying to get rid of me—at least I don't think so. But he saw something in me that I didn't see myself. Up to that point, I had completely resisted the notion of becoming a senior pastor. I saw the toll that ministry often took on people and, frankly, I didn't want to run the risk of that happening to my family and me.

Steve invited me to attend a celebration marking the thirty-fifth anniversary of his ordination. I went because Darel and his family were there. During a program after the dinner, various people from Steve's previous churches spoke and gave presentations, thanking him for the way God had changed their lives and congregations through his service as their pastor. During this program, God suddenly gave me a passion to be a pastor like Steve—someone whom God could use to lead and influence His Church.

The next day when Maria and I went out for dinner, I asked her if we should be open to leaving Calvary so that I could become a senior pastor. Once again, she nearly fainted from shock! We figured we would be safe for a while, because no church would call a youth and family guy to be their senior pastor. I spent time talking with mentors and creating a profile for the type of church that my gift set would best match. Maria and I remained in denial, thinking that my becoming a senior pastor would be down the road at least a few years.

We occasionally did a little searching on the Willow Creek Association's website to see if any churches with senior pastor openings fit my very narrow profile. One day, I came home from work and Maria said that she had found a church that was "very interesting."

"Where is it?" I asked.

"Ventura, California."

I wasn't expecting her to drop that bomb on me! I realize that for most people, the idea of leaving the cold of Minneapolis to head to the warm and sunny climate of Ventura, California, would seem like a no-brainer. But this was completely outside anything we had ever imagined. We're both Midwesterners, and our entire family lives in Minnesota, Iowa and Illinois. The idea of leaving behind everyone and everything we knew was terrifying.

As I filled out the application and sent my résumé, I figured we would never hear back from them. Yet even though the church received more than 125 applications for the position, somehow my résumé rose to the surface. God was undeniably at work, and in the fall of 2002, I left what I thought was my dream position at Calvary to become the senior pastor of Ventura Missionary Church (VMC).

For the past five years, I've had the opportunity to take the passion and vision for seeing faith lived out at home into my role as senior pastor. Today, I'm incredibly thankful that God brought me to VMC, because I couldn't ask for a more patient, caring and committed body to serve. God has given me a greater appreciation and understanding for the struggles senior pastors face as they faithfully try to lead their congregations where God wants them to lead. I have so much more to learn, and in no way do I consider myself an expert. Yet, at the very least, I now have a perspective that I didn't have before.

God Thing 6: A Faith at Home Movement
When I became senior pastor at VMC, I figured I would be leaving my youth and family calling to put on a new hat. Of course, I would bring my passion and commitment to be a faith at home church to VMC, because it was one of the reasons they called me. Yet I presumed I would no longer be helping other churches make faith at home a top priority. Little did I know that God had another plan in place.

Shortly after I arrived at VMC, I gave a sermon titled "Home as Church Too." I used the text of Deuteronomy 6 and quoted some statistics from George Barna that supported my message. After one of the services, a member of the church approached me. "Pastor Mark, I really appreciated your message," he said. "The statistics you shared from George Barna were very revealing. Did you know that he lives in Ventura? He occasionally attends VMC, and his daughter is enrolled in our school."

My jaw almost hit the floor! George Barna was a nationally and internationally recognized best-selling author of more than 35 books and the director of The Barna Group, a marketing research company that specializes in research for Christian ministries. For years, I had been using the research of The Barna Group. George had even once interviewed me over the phone as a part of the research he did for *Transforming Children into Spiritual Champions*, yet we'd never met. The next thing I knew, I was having lunch with him, and we started getting together every month or so just to share ideas with each other.

After I had been at VMC for a little more than a year, George encouraged me at one of our meetings to write a book for parents that would inspire, motivate and equip them to bring Christ and Christlike living into their homes. While I appreciated his encouragement, I had no clue where to start.

Then George said, "Did you know that Gospel Light is located in Ventura and that Bill and Rhonni Greig, who lead Gospel

Light, have three children in your school? Tell them I'll write the foreword, and see what they say." Interestingly, Maria and I were coaching a sixth-grade girls' basketball team at our school and the Greigs' daughter was on our team! To make a long story short, Gospel Light published *Faith Begins at Home* and this book, as well as a guide that provides resources to help churches launch faith at home movements in their congregations.

God, in a way that only He can work, had brought together a pastor whom He had instilled with a personal passion and vision, along with one of the nation's leading Christian researchers, and a publishing house to create a movement that would inspire, motivate and equip parents, pastors and church leaders to bring faith back into the home. However, something was still missing: a way to share this vision with pastors.

God Thing 7: A Faith at Home Broadcast Center

While I was writing my first book, I received a phone call from the Willow Creek Association asking me to be a keynote speaker at two upcoming conferences in Canada. Although I had attended numerous Willow Creek conferences, I had never been asked to be a keynote speaker. In fact, I was always blown away by the caliber of their speakers. Every time I heard Bill Hybels deliver his "The Local Church Is the Hope of the World" keynote address, I always walked away thinking I could conquer the world!

The caller from the Willow Creek Association said, "The first conference we would like you to speak at is the Promiseland Conference." The conference at least fit within my comfort zone, because most of the 1,000-plus attendees would be children's ministry pastors. I was used to talking in front of this kind of audience, and children's pastors generally were very warm, encouraging and accepting.

Then the Willow Creek representative dropped a bomb: "We would also like you to be a keynote speaker at the Acts 2 conference following Bill Hybels and Andy Stanley," she said. After I picked myself up off the floor, I realized that God was up to something greater than anything I had ever dreamed of! I now had an opportunity to share the passion and conceptual model that God had given me—and encourage more than 500 senior pastors and leaders to launch faith at home movements in their congregations.

Obviously, with all of my two-and-a-half years of senior pastor experience, I felt incredibly nervous and completely in over my head. I surrendered myself and the talk to God, went on stage, and gave it all I had. In yet another sign that God was clearly up to something, when evaluations about the conferences came in a few months later, the talks I gave on making faith at home a church's top priority were the highest rated. Now, I know that I'm not nearly the public communicator that Bill Hybels or Andy Stanley is, so it was clear that the faith at home message, vision and conceptual model resonated with church leaders. Since then, the Willow Creek Association has committed to helping lead this movement by serving as a broadcast center through the conferences they offer all around the world.

What Does This All Mean?

Why have I spent so much time taking you through my personal journey? Because I want you to see that the faith at home movement is about God and what He has done to give me the passion I have for families. At one point, I didn't own or use a set of faith at home lenses. But God changed me and put faith at home on my radar as a pastor. I still don't consider myself to be an expert; instead, I would describe myself as a practitioner who is personally invested in helping churches establish and equip homes to be the center of Christlike living. I firmly believe that home is the primary place where faith is nurtured and that parents should be the primary nurturers of faith.

As a result of my own experiences, I now recognize that the majority of today's families have no idea how to make their home a place for nurturing the faith of their children. Therefore, I want to come alongside them and help equip them to bring the love of Jesus Christ into the center of their homes and family life. I believe that only this will lead to families being healthy and strong. As a result, churches will be healthy and strong as well.

I firmly believe that God is at work leading a faith at home movement and that He will lead this movement in and through pastors who are called to serve His Church. I think God is growing tired of the hold Satan has had on families and that He is beginning to awaken pastors to this reality because He desires to reclaim every home. Having people attend church and "play" Christian for two hours on Sunday morning isn't good enough for God. He wants to be a part of our everyday lives. He's not going to rest—and neither should we—until He is a permanent part of our lives at home, work and play!

God changed me. He helped me to see things from a new perspective—the home—that I had completely overlooked. Maybe this is a perspective God wants to give you as well. May the Lord bless you as you prayerfully consider this new perspective.

Let's Get Personal

As I've talked with pastors about making faith at home the priority in their churches, I've learned that one thing that keeps many pastors from being passionate about this movement is the struggle of making faith the priority in their own homes. They feel guilty and wonder how they can lead something they aren't doing themselves.

As I've talked with pastors, many have confessed that they don't take the time to pray with their families or lead their families in Bible reading or devotions. Many have said, "I deal with that at work all day and I don't have the time or energy to do it at home." I admit that I also fall prey to this. In fact, Maria is more responsible for leading faith at home in our family than I am. Yet I know that God wants me to do whatever I can to keep Christ in the center of our home. His Word commands it:

> Hear, O Israel: The Lord our God, the Lord is one. Love the Lord your God with all your heart and with all your soul and with all your strength. These commandments that I give you today are to be upon your hearts. Impress them on your children (Deut. 6:7).

We looked at part of this passage in chapter 1, but here I want to point out what comes immediately before the words "impress them on your children." The instruction reads, "These commandments are to be upon *your* hearts" (emphasis added). Similarly, Joshua 24:15 says "as for me" before it says "and my household, we will serve the Lord." Scripture is clear—we can't pass on something to our churches that we don't have ourselves.

The whole movement to bring Christ and Christlike living back into the center of our homes is about *us* and *our* passion and commitment.

Starting in Your Home

I want to assure you that committing to and becoming passionate about this movement isn't all work with no reward. In fact, one of the greatest blessings in leading this movement in your church will be the benefit you and your own family will receive as you lead in your own home. Being a faith at home-driven pastor has made me a better husband and father in my own home because I am now held accountable for living out what I preach. I wouldn't be the husband and father that I am if faith at home wasn't a top priority for my church and me.

When Malyn was between two and three years old, Maria and I attended a Take It Home event at our church called "The Family Blessing" (you'll read more about these kinds of events in chapter 3). Neither Maria nor I really had any idea what blessing one's child meant. After receiving some biblical teaching about the significance of parents blessing their children, the event leaders introduced Rolf Garborg, author of *The Family Blessing*.[4]

Rolf told us that he had started a ritual of saying a blessing over his daughter every evening. When she was an infant, he would go into her room as she was sleeping and say, "May the Lord continue to bless you and keep you. May the Lord continue to make His face shine on you and be gracious to you. May the Lord continue to look upon you with favor and give you peace. In the name of the Father, and the Son and the Holy Spirit. I love you. Amen."

As Rolf's daughter grew older, he continued the blessing ritual, even through her teenage years. He admits that during one period of time when she was a teenager, he would again wait until she was asleep to give her the blessing. But he kept up the ritual.

Rolf and his wife dreaded the day when they would have to leave their daughter at college. To make it through that day, they came up with a plan to unload her stuff, quickly say their goodbyes in the dorm room, grab each other's hands and head for the car with no looking back. The plan worked to perfection—until they were almost to their car. In the distance behind them, they heard their daughter cry, "Mom! Dad! Wait!"

Rolf and his wife stopped in their tracks and turned around to see their daughter come running up after them. With tears in her eyes, she said, "You forgot to bless me." Right there in the parking lot, they huddled together and said, "May the Lord continue to bless you and keep you. May the Lord continue to make His face shine on you and be gracious to you. May the Lord continue to look upon you with favor and give you peace. In the name of the Father, and the Son and the Holy Spirit. I love you. Amen."

Guess what Maria and I started doing immediately after we heard this story? Now, every evening before Malyn goes to bed, Maria repeats this same blessing to her. Even if we're separated for an evening, Maria shares the blessing over the phone. There have even been occasions when Malyn has said, "Don't forget to bless me!"

My daughter, now 11, has been hearing this blessing every evening since she was 2 years old. Recently, as I was leaving for a trip to speak in Canada, I went into Malyn's room at 4 A.M. to give her a kiss goodbye. I didn't think she would wake up, but to my surprise she did. When she saw me, she reached out her arm from underneath the covers, extended it to me and in a groggy, half-awake voice said, "Daddy, as you go on your trip, may the Lord bless you and keep you. May the Lord make His face shine on you and be gracious to you. May the Lord look upon you with favor and give you peace. In the name of the Father, and the Son and the Holy Spirit. I love you, Daddy! Amen."

A Blessing for You

This is just an example of what can happen when we make faith at home a top priority in our churches by making it a top priority in our own homes. We'll be the ones who are blessed! I didn't come up with the family blessing at the Take It Home event at our church—someone else who had been infected with this vision did. Yet Maria and I were the beneficiaries of it.

I think that's the Church at its very best! Imagine what could happen to your church if parts of the church body—men's ministry, women's ministry, adult ministry, children's ministry, youth ministry, small-group ministry, senior adult ministry and so on—all came alongside one another to help bring Christ and Christlike living into its members' homes. If this were to take place, I believe that many of the problems we face as church leaders would go away.

May the Lord bless you as you faithfully provide leadership in your church that will help bring Christ back into the center of your family and every family in your church.

Ponder, Pray and Discuss

1. Did you have a faith-filled home growing up? Did you have parents who set an example of Christlike living for you? Did you pray as a family? Did you attend church and participate in church programs together? Did your parents talk with you about faith or give you a Bible? If you experienced any of these things, take a moment to thank God for your upbringing. You might want to send a thank-you note to your parents, because what you've experienced isn't normal.

2. What about your home life now? Would an outsider describe it as a faith-filled home? How would your children describe it? As a parent, do you try to set an example of Christlike living for your children? Do you pray as a family? Do you talk with your children about faith? Of course, you're a busy pastor and you're at church a lot, but do you ever serve in a ministry together as a family?

3. As you reflect on your family's faith life growing up and your own family's faith life now, how do these experiences affect your view of family ministry in the church?

4. If you could take one small step today to bring Christ back into the center of your own family, what would it be? What's stopping you from taking that step?

CHAPTER 3 SUMMARY:

- How churches can equip the home to be the main place where faith is nurtured.

- How existing ministry structures in your church can equip families for building faith at home.

- The biblical call to equip families to live out faith at home.

- Contemporary calls for making faith at home a top priority in the Church.

- Tangible steps to take to become a faith at home pastor and church.

- The weakness of "add a silo" family ministry.

- The strength of being a "church *of* family" ministry.

- How Take It Home events inspire, provide practice for faith skills and equip families to take home the skills.

- How a meaningful series of Take It Home events can become a string weaving together all that your church does.

- The cumulative and transformational effects of Take It Home events.

- Ways to extend faith at home vision beyond children, youth and family ministry.

- The fun of tweaking what you already do in your own church.

- *Remember:* You can do it!

What Should We Do About It?

One of the most serious tasks of the church at large is to help its member families to be the body of Christ within the home—to become settings where unconditional love, affirmation, challenge to accountability, and forgiveness are known; to learn and share rituals, symbols, and stories of faith; to recognize and claim their special gifts and mission in the world.[1]

Marjorie Thompson

Deena and her husband were the parents of two beautiful children, one aged nine and the other just a few months old. Deena had been moved by one of my messages regarding the role parents play in passing on faith to their children and had made a personal commitment to bring Christ into the center of her life and the life of her family. She called me and set up a time to have her younger child dedicated.

Just a week before the dedication, Deena called to tell me that her baby had died of SIDS. The loss was devastating, and I continued to pray for Deena as I knew how difficult this would be for her. Two months later, Deena came to a baptism class that I was leading. When it came time for her to share her personal testimony, the class was blown away. She tearfully, yet calmly, shared about the loss of her baby and how painful it had been for her. But she went on to tell how much more important God had become to her as a result.

Deena said that the church had carried her through the difficult days. She was overwhelmed by the love the people of the church had showered on her and her family. She was thankful that she had come to know God's love for her before this tragedy occurred and that she knew He was her source of strength and peace. Now, she wanted to be baptized to publicly show that despite her pain and her unanswered questions, God would continue to be the most important thing in her life and in the life of her family.

On the Sunday that Deena was baptized, there wasn't a dry eye in the place! Two years later, God blessed Deena and her husband with another child. Deena has repeatedly said, "I really don't know what I would have done without God and this church. We didn't even know many of these people personally, but they carried us through. They showered us with the love of Christ when we needed it most."

I can't tell you what might have happened to Deena and her family if she hadn't had Christ in her life during this difficult time. Yet I know for certain that she and her family would not have the peace and joy they now have if Christ and the church hadn't come alongside them in their time of need.

Where We Are

Let's pause a minute to recap. We've determined that God is calling the Church to rise up and address the area that Satan is attacking the most: our families. At the same time, we've learned that parents today want to have a better family than the one they grew up in. And we've concluded that it's time for the Church to come alongside families and equip them to bring Christ into the center of their homes.

If that's where we are, what's next? We now face the challenge—and the opportunity—of determining how we can equip the home to be the primary place where faith is nurtured and how that equipping can take place through our existing ministry structures.

When I was growing up, my dad would often repeat an expression that you've probably heard: "You can either be part of the problem or part of the solution." These words certainly apply as we face the reality that Christlike living isn't happening in our homes today in spite of some of the best programs the Church has ever offered. As church leaders, we can either be part of the problem or part of the solution. In other words, we can either continue enabling this to happen or we can do something about it.

In the last chapter, I told you about my personal journey that led me to establish a faith at home movement. When I learned that parents are two to three times more influential in passing on faith to their children than any church program, I knew that I had to make some changes. At that point in my ministry, I was spending 99.9 percent of my time focusing on things that were happening at the church. Of course, this left little or no time to focus on helping equip homes to be the primary place where faith is nurtured.

Like a lot of pastors, I used to define success as more people coming to more activities at the church so that we could build more buildings that would enable us to offer more events for more people at church! Whew—what a rat race! To be honest, I wasn't even aware that I needed to be concerned with what was taking place in homes. I had no idea that less than 10 percent of the people in my church were praying, reading the Bible or doing devotions in their homes.[2] I had no idea that the majority of parents had abdicated their faith-nurturing responsibilities to us, the "experts," through our programs.

Yet the glassy stares I received on Sunday mornings as I made suggestions for what parents could do in their weekly devotions should have told me all I needed to know. When I witnessed what was happening in families at our church on a weekly basis and watched the divorce rate among Christian couples in America climb as high or even a little higher than the overall divorce rate, I shouldn't have been surprised that these types of things weren't taking place in the home.[3]

A Biblical Mandate

When I speak to pastors about this issue, I find that they're usually not shocked by the information about the condition of families. The situation might be a bit worse than they thought, but they still aren't too surprised. A person doesn't have to be in ministry very long to realize that Christlike living isn't happening in homes today.

It also doesn't take a lot of convincing for church leaders to realize that parents are far more influential than church programs. And most pastors realize, as the following passages clearly show, that God intends and calls us to equip families to live out faith at home:

- For I have chosen [Abraham], so that he will direct his children and his household after him to keep the way of the Lord (Gen. 18:19).

- Train a child in the way he should go, and when he is old he will not turn from it (Prov. 22:6).

- These commandments that I give you today are to be upon your hearts. Impress them on your children. Talk about them when you sit at home and when you walk along the road, when you lie down and when you get up. Tie them as symbols on your hands and bind them on your foreheads. Write them on the doorframes of your houses and on your gates (Deut. 6:6-9).

• But if serving the Lord seems undesirable to you, then choose for yourselves this day whom you will serve, whether the gods your forefathers served beyond the River, or the gods of the Amorites, in whose land you are living. But as for me and my household, we will serve the Lord (Josh. 24:15).

• He decreed statutes for Jacob and established the law in Israel, which he commanded our forefathers to teach their children, so the next generation would know them, even the children yet to be born, and they in turn would tell their children. Then they would put their trust in God and would not forget his deeds but would keep his commands (Ps. 78:5-8).

• Children, obey your parents in the Lord, for this is right. "Honor your father and mother"—which is the first commandment with a promise—"that it may go well with you and that you may enjoy long life on the earth." Fathers, do not exasperate your children; instead, bring them up in the training and instruction of the Lord (Eph. 6:1-4).

Other Voices

The faith at home crisis is a reality. Take a look at just a few of the many leaders who are emphasizing the need for faith at home to be a top priority in the church:

• *Tom Schultz, Group Publishing:* "If you're not doing family ministry, you're not doing youth ministry."

This quote appeared on the front cover of a 1995 issue of *Group* magazine. At the time, Group Publishing had very few family ministry resources. Since then, the company has woven family ministry and faith at home components into much of their materials and resources.

• *Larry Fowler, Director of AWANA Clubs International:* "Research consistently affirms the declining biblical worldview (a perspective of life grounded in biblical truth) of our young people. It is nothing short of a crisis, even among committed Christian families! What will stop it? There is very little anyone can do, unless the home (and hence the parents) are involved at the core."[4] For many years, AWANA Clubs International was an effective yet church-based children's ministry program. AWANA has made a significant change in their methodology to become more faith at home intentional through their AWANA clubs.

• *Roland Martinson, Luther Seminary:* "The church's role is to be equippers of families. What we ought to do is let the kids drop their parents off at church, train the parents and send them back to their mission field, their home, to grow Christians." Dr. Martinson has boldly led the way in developing a seminary training program for pastors that focuses on faith at home.

• *Marjorie Thompson, Director of Pathways Center for Christian Spirituality:* "The family, more than any other context of life, is the foundational place of spiritual formation in its broad sense, especially for children. If the church wishes to see the content of this formation as explicitly Christian, it will need to take the role and support of the family far more seriously than it has."[5] Marjorie Thompson, an ordained minister in the Presbyterian Church (USA), has a long-standing interest in the area of spiritual formation. Her book *The Family as Forming Center* was originally published in 1996 in response to a consultation on family spirituality sponsored by The Upper Room. The consultation was both timely and ahead of its time, as the level of interest in the role of families has risen dramatically since then—both in church and in culture.

- *Christian Smith and Melinda Denton, Sociologists of Religion:* "In sum, therefore, we think that the best general rule of thumb that parents might use to reckon their children's most likely religious outcomes is this: 'We'll get what we are.' By normal processes of socialization, and unless other significant forces intervene, more than what parents might say they want as religious outcomes in their children, most parents most likely will end up getting religiously of their children what they themselves are."[6] Smith and Denton's book *Soul Searching* offers one of the most comprehensive studies on the religious and spiritual lives of American teenagers and clearly identifies the critical need for faith at home.

In fact, these contemporary calls for making faith at home a top priority in the Church simply echo what preacher, theologian and missionary Jonathan Edwards realized in the American colonial era: "Every Christian family ought to be as it were a little church consecrated to Christ, and wholly influenced and governed by his rule."[7]

Getting Practical

As I travel and speak, I spend less time trying to convince pastors and church leaders that a faith at home problem exists. Instead, I find myself focusing the majority of my time on what we can do about it. That's what we're going to do now—provide some tangible steps that you can take to become a faith at home pastor and church. It's time to get to work! Or, as Ty Pennington from the television show *Extreme Makeover: Home Edition* says, "Let's do it!"

Extreme Faith at Home Makeover

In America, we've become very good at building and rebuilding houses. In a matter of months, an open field that previously produced a crop of corn can become a housing development with a crop of hundreds of houses. The rebuilding boom might have reached its highest level ever with the TV show mentioned above, *Extreme Makeover: Home Edition*. On the show, host and carpenter Ty Pennington leads a team to rebuild or replace the dilapidated homes of needy families. In just a week's time, the team and an army of local builders completely rebuild a home, often making it one of the nicest homes in the community.

The first few minutes of each episode focus on the dilapidated home and introduce viewers to the family in need. By the end of this segment, those watching see the horrible condition of the home. After meeting the family members and hearing their story, viewers begin to have a personal desire to see the family's condition changed. From that point forward, the planning and work begin to rebuild the home.

While we've become adept at rebuilding houses, we need an extreme makeover when it comes to establishing Christ into the center of every home. In chapter 1, we looked at the dilapidated condition families are in today. In chapter 2, we looked at some of the blessings you and your church will receive if you make changing this condition your top priority. Now, it's time to roll up our sleeves and get to work.

The "Add a Silo" Model

On *Extreme Makeover: Home Edition*, the first thing the team does is create a new vision and design for a home that will meet the needs of the family they're helping. Let's take a look at a new vision for family ministry that could help us reestablish the home as the primary place where faith is nurtured.

Over the past 15 years, as churches have become more aware of the need for strong family ministry, two types of family ministry models have appeared. The first I call the "add a silo" family ministry model. With this model, a church approaches family ministry the same way it approaches everything else—through programs. The infants and toddlers go into the nursery program, the three-year-olds through sixth-graders go into the Sunday School program, the junior and senior highers end up in the youth ministry program, and the adults get placed into the adult Sunday School or into another small-group ministry. Each silo develops a program approach to grow and pass on the faith to those within its ministry.

So, when a church wakes up to the reality that it needs to focus on families, it takes the same approach and simply adds a silo (program) called "family ministry." The church creates a family ministry team that organizes family game nights, family camps, family retreats, family date nights, and many other creative family programs.

Unfortunately, I have found that even with the best of intentions and efforts, these family ministry programs typically result in a turnout of only 4 out of 10 families. I know this is the case because I've tried family ministry programs this way myself! Even when we offered an event with the nation's best speakers and I used every promotional tool available, only about

40 percent of our families would attend. And most of those who attended were already passing on the faith in their homes and didn't need the help! We were trying to add another activity to an already-too-busy calendar of events and weren't reaching the parents and families who truly needed to be trained and equipped to bring Christ into the center of their homes.

Add a Silo

While the add-a-silo model is clearly the most predominant model for family ministry—because it represents what we know how to do—it isn't the most effective. If we want to bring true transformation to more families, we must embrace a comprehensive and integrated approach to family ministry and become churches *of* family ministry.

The "Church *of* Family Ministry" Model

For the last 25 years or so, the Church has gone through a significant discipleship transformation as a result of the small-group ministry movement. How effective this movement has been in individual churches seems to be connected to the approach each church takes to small-group ministry.

Maybe you've heard the catchphrase attached to the small-group movement: "You can be a church *with* small groups or you can be a church *of* small groups." Interestingly, this is just another way of saying that you can take a program approach to small-group ministry by adding a separate small-group program to everything else and produce a marginal impact, or you can make small groups an integrated part of how you do ministry as a church and exponentially increase the effectiveness of the transformation in people's lives.

In the same way, you can be a church *with* a family ministry—the add-a-silo model—and have marginal impact. Or you can adopt the "church *of* family" model and learn to look at everything your church does through lenses of bringing faith and Christlike living back into the center of every family.

A Church *of* Family Ministry

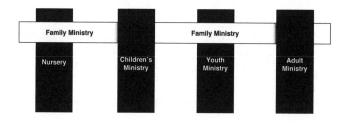

With a church *of* family ministry model, instead of adding family ministry to the children's ministry director's job description, the goal of every ministry of the church is to equip the home to be the primary place where faith is nurtured. In a church *of* family ministry, you appropriately elevate family ministry to be a part of how you do church. It looks something like this:

- Your men's and women's ministries equip men and women to live out their faith at home.

- Your small-group ministry focuses on equipping people and holds them accountable for living out their faith in their homes.
- Your prayer ministry equips every family to pray daily in their homes instead of focusing on a few big prayer events at the church.
- Your sermons include an emphasis on taking the message home and living it out on a daily basis.
- Your church's Bible studies equip adults to be like Christ in their homes, community and world.
- Your children's ministry helps equip parents to talk with their children about faith.
- Your youth ministry helps parents keep their teenagers engaged in a walk with the Lord through ongoing faith talk in the home.

Notice that these ministries focus on what is happening in the *home*, not what is happening at *church*.

Whole New Vision or Just New Lenses?

Another way of looking at faith at home family ministry is not to think of it as a whole new vision but as a new set of lenses. Once your church puts on these lenses, it will begin to view its ministries in a completely different way. This new way of looking at things will dramatically impact the vision of your church.

Please hear me when I say that the last thing your church needs to fix the faith at home problem is a whole new program. There is no new program out there that will fix the faith at home problem. Rather, this problem can only be corrected when your church takes active steps to correct its "eyesight" problem that has been preventing it from fully making its vision come into focus. I believe that God provides each church with a clear vision. Your church might not need to change its vision or strategy, but in order to be the church God wants you to be, you might need to put on the faith at home lenses so that your church can clearly see that vision become a reality.

Satan knows just how strong the Church can be when its members gather together around a common vision. It's like grabbing a handful of pencils and trying to break them all at once—not very easy to do. However, if Satan can divide the families in the Church, it becomes more like breaking a single pencil—which is a lot easier for him to do. So Satan keeps churches from achieving their vision by breaking families and getting faith out of the home. And remember, a family today might consist of a single person living in a nursing home or a 21-year-old college student living in an apartment as easily as it might consist of a mom, dad and 2.5 children. As I mentioned in chapter 1, a *USA Today* article states that there are at least 28 different forms of families that exist today. Most churches probably have most of those forms of the family represented.

Therefore, without your faith at home lenses on, your church's vision for the elderly woman or the college student can't be fully realized. The home is the place where your vision as a church will be carried out. We've mistakenly thought that the church vision gets carried out at church, but it doesn't.

This church *of* family ministry vision shouldn't be difficult for us to embrace. It's the way the church used to operate. The catechism was developed as an instructional tool for parents to pass on the basic teachings of the Church to their children. George Barna describes it in *Revolution*:

Christian families taught the ways of God in their homes every day. Parents were expected to model a Spirit-led lifestyle for their children, and families were to make their home a sanctuary for God. In a very real sense, the home was the early church—supplemented by larger gatherings in the Temple and elsewhere, but never replaced by what took place in the homes of believers.[8]

Therefore, in some ways we need to return to the way things used to be in order to reestablish the home as the primary place where faith is nurtured.

Uniquely Designed

On *Extreme Makeover: Home Edition*, the team bases its vision and design for the new home on the needs and personalities of the family members themselves. One child might have a love for basketball, so the designers create his room to look like a basketball court. Another child might love nature and tree houses, so her room has a lofted bed that appears to be in a tree house! The designers think, plan and create everything through the lenses of the family members themselves. When the family comes home, they have the greatest house in the world because it has been designed specifically for them. Imagine if the Church looked at faith in the home in the same way: to help each unique family bring Christ and Christlike living back into the center of their home so that they could have the greatest home environment in the world!

As I mentioned in the previous chapter, I grew up at a Bible camp. While we had a pretty awesome backyard, our home itself wasn't very nice. It was actually two 15-plus-year-old mobile homes connected by an unheated enclosed entryway that also served as our laundry and storage room and my Nerf basketball court! In fact, we probably would have qualified for *Extreme Makeover* ourselves! Yet I have only positive memories and feelings about that home. We had Jesus in our home, and that made it the best place to live in the world!

Just think what would happen if instead of focusing on what our church buildings look like, we focused on what our homes and families look like. Of course, we might not like what we see. Becoming a church *of* family ministry is messy business because our families—no matter what shape, size or age—are a mess.

However, if we have a Matthew 28 vision to "go into all nations," we need to realize that the journey to all nations begins by taking Jesus into our homes! How can we take something into the world that we haven't even taken home? We can't. That's why faith at home must be a top priority in the Church.

A "Show Me" Starting Point

The rebuilt homes on *Extreme Makeover* still have bathrooms, bedrooms, a kitchen and so forth, yet they end up very different than how they started. As I stated earlier, I don't think the Church needs to get rid of Sunday School, youth ministry, men's ministry and other programs. Instead, we need to rethink how to do these ministries through our faith at home lenses. So, what do existing ministries such as nursery, Sunday School, youth ministry, small-group ministry and others look like in a faith at home-focused church? Let's take a look.

Instilling Faith at Home Through Sunday School

One of the greatest challenges we face in the church where I pastor is getting parents to show up for faith at home training and equipping events. What if I told you that we've discovered how to get a 98 percent turnout rate for events that equip parents to pass on the faith themselves? Would that pique your interest? Well, that's exactly what we've been able to do. Here's how.

We begin by asking ourselves what faith skills every family should be equipped to practice in their homes. In other words, we ask ourselves what an "as for me and my household we will serve the Lord" family looks like. Before long, we have a healthy list of activities and disciplines such as prayer, Bible reading, devotions, blessings, family service projects, and so on.

After we compile the list, we determine at what age each faith skill should be taught in the home so that it can be firmly established. For example, it probably wouldn't be a good idea for parents to wait until their children are teenagers before they start the ritual of blessing them. However, if parents start the ritual of blessing before a child turns five, it can become an established practice that continues through the teenage years and beyond.

Armed with our list of faith skills and predetermined ages for when each skill should be established, we then put together a faith at home training and equipping workshop for each specific faith skill. We call our family training and equipping workshops "Take It Home" events. Instead of scheduling them for an additional time that families would need to come to church, we built them into our Sunday School and youth ministry programs. This makes it much easier for parents to participate in the events, because they take place during times when they are already bringing their children to church.

At least once each year, we ask the parents to attend Sunday School with their children. On that day, parents learn a new faith skill that they can immediately implement in their home. Over time, families began to anticipate upcoming Take It Home events, because they know they will receive training to help them as a family.

Take It Home Basics
Take It Home events can vary in length based on a congregation's approach to children's and youth ministry. A typical Take It Home event includes a time of worship, inspirational teaching time, interactive activity, parent/child discussion time

(usually in small groups with two or three other families), and a take-home resource. The take-home resource is an important tool because it helps families continue what they learned at the Take It Home event in their homes.

There are three main purposes of the Take It Home event. First, through the use of biblical teaching and personal testimonies, families are inspired to want to do the faith skill at home. Second, families see how to do the faith skill in an active learning manner and are encouraged to experience doing the faith skill together as a family. Third, families are equipped to continue doing the faith skill in their home and are provided with a resource that enables them to do so.

Other Take It Home Events

The *Take It Home* implementation guide that I coauthored with Dave Teixeira provides complete outlines for 14 Take It Home events that you can customize for your church.[9] Let me share a few examples of Take It Home events so that you can better understand how they help bring the faith at home vision into your church's ministry.

Infant Dedication/Baptism (for Parents of Infants/Newborns)

Infant dedication or baptism can either be a ritual we perform in our churches or it can be treated as the beginning of a life-long partnership. As a performed ritual, a dedication or baptism will have very little lasting impact. Yet if we seize the opportunity, it can become a powerful first step in establishing the parents as the most important faith influencers, the home as the primary place where faith is nurtured, and the Church as a lifelong partner in equipping parents to pass on faith to their children.

When we have a dedication at the church where I serve, we ask the parents, grandparents and sponsors to all come forward with the child being dedicated.[10] We take a moment to remind the parents that they will primarily be responsible for passing on faith to their child. We then ask them if they will accept and follow through with this responsibility.

We then explain the role of the church: Together with the grandparents and godparents, we will come alongside the parents as lifelong partners to help equip them and hold them accountable. We then ask the church, grandparents and godparents to accept that responsibility.

Following the dedication, we present to the family a wooden faith chest made by some men in our congregation.[11] We explain that over the course of the child's life, the church, grandparents and godparents will provide faith-building resources that the parents can use to teach their child about Jesus and His love.

We conclude by explaining that the parents' goal should be to fill the faith chest while raising the child so that when he or she has a child, he or she can have all the resources needed to pass on the faith. Inside the faith chest, we include a copy of *Faith Begins at Home*. Dedication or infant baptism provides a perfect first opportunity to establish the home and parents as the primary influencers of faith.

My Bible Take It Home Event

Every year, our church had the same tradition. On a Sunday morning each October, the third-graders marched up to the front of the worship area. The pastor called each child forward and personally presented a Bible to him or her. After all the children received their Bibles, the congregation applauded and the children left the sanctuary.

Don't get me wrong—this was okay. I obviously liked the idea of the church providing a Bible for each third-grader. Yet after I became infected with the faith at home vision, I remember asking a simple question: "How does this help bring Bible reading into the home?"

So the next year, we decided to have a Take It Home event called My Bible one week before the Bible presentation Sunday. Parents accompanied their third-graders to this event. On each table, we placed two or three old Bibles that belonged to some of our senior adults. The pages throughout were written on and various passages were highlighted. Instantly, the kids were drawn to the Bibles and the handwritten notes.

We took some time to teach families about the basics of the Bible, the difference between the Old and New Testaments, and why reading the Word of God is so important. We then gave the kids an opportunity to pick out a new Bible and allowed them to sit down at their tables and make personalized Bible covers. We knew this craft activity would keep most of the kids busy for a while.

As the students worked on their Bible covers, we took the parents to a different room and introduced them to Mr. Reinhardt. Mr. Reinhardt, who's about 70 years old, shared that he received a Bible from his dad when he was in third grade. He explained that inside the front cover of the Bible was a personal note his dad had written him. Before he read the note to the parents, he explained how important it was to him. "About a year after my dad gave me this Bible, he was killed in a farming accident," Mr. Reinhardt said. "My dad was a man of few words, but this note has been the one thing that has kept me close to him all these years." When he read the note his dad had written, many of the parents cried. So did I.

After a few moments of reflection, we asked the parents to write a note in their children's new Bibles. Believe me, they wrote serious notes! The following Sunday, instead of simply marching the kids forward, we invited the parents to come to the front with their third-graders. We presented the Bible to the parents and explained that this was part of the church's role in coming alongside them. In turn, the parents presented the Bibles to their children, and the third-graders opened their Bibles to read for the first time the personal notes written inside. For many of the students, it was the first time they had ever received a personal note from their parents.

Inside the back cover of the Bible, we provided a Bible reading guide that the kids could use to highlight two verses a day during the coming year. We also gave them a challenge: "Maybe one day, your Bible can look like the Bibles you saw last week in your classroom!" You could tell by looking at the eyes of these third-graders that they were up to the challenge! Over the course of the next year, those Bibles were used and highlighted in the homes!

The idea for this event involved taking an event the church was already doing and adding a layer that equipped faith to happen at home. If we want families to read the Bible in their homes, we need to do our part to inspire, motivate and equip them to do it.

The Next Steps

Imagine what would happen if every family attended a Take It Home event each year from the birth of their child until that child reached age 18. In one church I served, we held 22 Take It Home events each year. This meant that some parents had to come to 2 events per year, which they were glad to do because these events made them better families of faith. Here's an example of how a series of Take It Home events could lay out during a child's years at home. Remember, these events take place on different Sundays throughout the year.

TARGET AGE	EVENT	WHAT IT TEACHES
Infants	Dedication/Infant Baptism	How Mom and Dad are primary faith influencers and the church is a lifelong partner
2-3	Family Blessings	How to ritually bless your child
3-4	Family Devotions	How to have family devotions
5-6	My Church	How to enjoy going to church
7-8	Prayer	How to pray together
8-9	Family Serve	How to do family service projects
9-10	My Bible	How to read the Bible together
10-11	Worship	How to worship together at home
11-12	Money and Me	How to manage your money
12-13	Computer and Music Boundaries	What is okay to look at/listen to and what is not
13-14	A Second Option	How to establish a Christian mentor
14-16	Dating, Kissing, Sex and Stuff	That true love waits
17-18	Looking into the Future	Spiritual gifts and following God

Take It Home events can be woven into Sunday School for younger kids, and as kids grow into teenagers, the Take It Home event can be added onto a youth ministry event. For example, Dave Teixeira served as one of my youth directors. Each year, he led a retreat for 12- to 14-year-olds for the "Dating, Kissing, Sex and Stuff" event listed above. He took the teenagers off to a weekend retreat at a Bible camp, where he taught and challenged them to make wise, biblical decisions as they prepared to enter into the dating years. Dave didn't hold back any punches. The retreat was always very influential and life changing for the teenagers who attended.

Inevitably, though, when the teens returned home from the retreat and got off the bus, Mom and Dad would be anxiously waiting, wondering how things had gone. The parents would ask their teen, "How was the retreat?" Even if the retreat had been the most life-changing experience that teen had ever had, his or her response would be simply, "It was okay." And that would be the end of the communication between parent and teen on this very important subject.

When Dave became infected with the faith at home vision, he faced a difficult realization. During all the years he had led the retreat, he had done so in an effort to help parents out by discussing a difficult topic with their teens. However, Dave now realized that by not involving parents, he was robbing them of an experience that could bring them closer together with their teenage sons and daughters. While most youth pastors would have scored this event a success because of the great attendance and the life-changing influence it had on the teens, Dave realized that the retreat, as currently formatted, was a failure. So he made a change to make the retreat an event that equipped parents to impart faith at home.

The next year, Dave brought the parents in two hours before the students returned from the retreat. He went through the teachings he had covered on the retreat and then provided questionnaires that parents could use to start a discussion with their teenagers. When the students arrived, Dave brought them together with their parents and led a final session. With their parents as witnesses, the students made commitments to abstain from sexual activity before marriage! Many parents thanked Dave for helping them have the discussion they knew they needed to have.

A Critical String

I hope these examples have helped provide a picture of what things can look like when you implement faith at home at your church. Establishing some sort of Take It Home strategy—

whether you call it that or not—that weaves through your children's and youth ministry is a critical step in becoming a church *of* family ministry.

The Take It Home events can become a string that weaves through and holds together all you do with children, youth and families. Without this string, it's easy for each ministry (silo) to run in its own direction. This leads to your church becoming program driven with a congregation spread a mile wide but with faith only an inch deep.

Many Sunday School curriculums have developed resources that children take home. Most publishers realize the critical importance of faith at home. Yet if parents aren't trained how to use these resources, what difference do they make? They just become another item for the trash bin. However, Take It Home events allow you to intentionally equip the home to be the primary place where faith is nurtured.

Too Simple?

I know that you might be thinking that this all seems too easy. How could one event per year lead to significant change? My response is simply that you are right; one event a year *won't* lead to significant change at home. But these aren't one-time-only events. They are training and equipping experiences!

None of the Take It Home events are designed to be one-time-only events. Each event has a specific purpose to inspire, motivate and equip families to begin a specific faith skill in their home that they will continue doing forever. You don't stop doing family prayer when you learn how to do family service. The Take It Home events have a cumulative effect as each one adds to the others. Another reason why this Take It Home strategy is so effective is the fact that each individual faith skill has the ability to transform families. Just getting a family to pray together can transform that family for Christ.

I know from experience that not every family will latch on to every faith skill taught at the Take It Home events. In our church, we hold an event each year to teach parents of 2- to 3-year-olds how to bless their children each evening. I know that not every parent will do this, although some do. The next year, we teach parents how to do family devotions together. Again, I know that not every family will do this on a consistent basis, but some do. Therefore, we consistently give families the opportunity to bring Christ and Christlike living into their home. Even if you took a cynical view and claimed that over the course of 14 years and 14 Take It Home events a family only actively engages in 3 faith skills, I would point out that at least they are doing 3 more than they were before!

Pick whatever 3 skills you want from the list on page 89 and tell me that a family doing these skills regularly at home won't be changed for Christ. You can't! A family managing its money in a godly way will be changed. A family serving others together for Christ will be changed. A family that finds a Christian mentor to interact in the life of the family will be changed.

If a Take It Home event becomes just another activity at church, it won't have the type of impact needed to change families. But if you invest in Take It Home events so that they become experiences that inspire, motivate and equip parents to do these faith skills in the home, you'll see transformed families in the long run.

Extending the Vision

Remember that the faith at home vision extends beyond children, youth and family ministry. Just think of what would happen if your entire church were to become infected with a faith at home vision:

- Your men's ministry would understand that the most important thing it does is to equip men to live out their faith and talk about it in their homes with their spouses and children.

- Your women's ministry would desire to equip women to practice faith at home, because it recognizes that moms are the top influencer in the faith development of children.

- Your senior adult ministry would engage seniors to meddle in the lives of their children and grandchildren because it's a God-given responsibility.

- Your outreach ministry would refocus what it does so that families could become involved in outreach as a family.

- Your preaching and teaching would provide more practical examples and personal challenges for Christlike living in the home. Fill-in-the-blank sermon notes would be changed to include a Take It Home section filled with questions to consider, application ideas to implement and additional Scriptures to study.

Just Some Tweaks

To make something a faith at home event, you might not need to make revolutionary changes. Maybe all you need to do is tweak something you're already doing—just a bit. The key to every Take It Home event is to intentionally equip families to do the faith skill and to invest in the families by giving them a resource to continue doing the faith skill in the home. You don't simply give them fish; you teach them how to fish.

For example, I knew of a church that had a sermon note program. The youth leader encouraged the junior high students to attend worship, fill out sermon notes and to turn them in following the service. The incentive was that the more sermon notes a student turned in, the larger the scholarship available for attending a week of Bible camp.

However, once this church became infected with the faith at home vision, they changed the sermon note forms to car time notes that the students worked through with their parents at home before turning in. This one simple change helped promote and increase faith talk in the home. When, as a church, you become infected with the faith at home vision, you'll look at all of your ministries in a different way. Maybe you'll be using a new set of lenses!

Recently, a group of pastors from different churches in Canada came to Ventura Missionary Church to meet with us and witness a Take It Home event. I'll never forget their comments at the end of the weekend: "What we love about what you're doing is the fact that there really isn't anything fancy about it. It's not like you need a fancy facility or charismatic leader to make it happen. Please don't take this wrong, but there is nothing spectacular about your church facility, yet the way you have woven the faith at home vision into how you do church is truly spectacular. This is something any church could do and that every church needs to do."

If you came to VMC during any given week, you wouldn't see some incredible program with dancing elephants or a building that absolutely wows you. Instead, you would see a normal church building. But what might set us apart is the fact that everything we do is aimed squarely at bringing faith back into the home.

You Can Do It!

Earlier in this chapter, we talked about the *Extreme Makeover: Home Edition* show. Perhaps a better analogy, if we want to stay in the building and design realm, is the catchphrase for Home Depot, the major do-it-yourself home improvement chain: "You Can Do It!"

It doesn't matter what size church you serve. It doesn't matter whether you pastor a mainline, evangelical, traditional, postmodern, build-the-believer or seeker-oriented church. It doesn't matter if you are Lutheran, Catholic, Presbyterian, Baptist, Evangelical Free or are non-denominational. We all face the same truth—the home is the primary place where faith is nurtured. Period.

My prayer is that the examples in this chapter will help you begin developing a model that will work in your congregation. I've served in four different churches, and the model has looked different in all four congregations. That is the strength of what I've provided for you—it's definitely not a program in a box that you can implement as is. I hope that what you've received is a set of faith at home lenses that will change, in varying degrees, the way you lead your church.

Remember, you can do it!

Some Insights from a Practitioner

The awareness of a need and the capacity to meet
that need: this constitutes a call.[1]
John Raleigh Mott

At this point, you're about halfway through this book. So let's take a break. Since you're still reading and I'm still writing, I would like to call this a "working lunch."

I'm hoping that you're not feeling defeated. Certainly, the thought of transforming your ministry and church into a place that equips the home to be the primary place where faith is nurtured can be overwhelming. So before moving on, let's spend a few moments listening to someone who has led this kind of faith at home movement through children, youth and family ministry.

Pastor Dave Teixeira serves as the children's, youth and family ministry pastor at Ventura Missionary Church, where I'm senior pastor. Dave and I have served together in two different congregations for a total of more than 10 years. (This alone qualifies him for sainthood!) Dave is primarily responsible for leading the faith at home movement at VMC. As I mentioned in the last chapter, Dave also coauthored a resource with me called *Take It Home,* an implementation guide filled with practical ideas and resources for making your church one that equips the home to be the main place where faith is nurtured.

Dave offers some important and useful insights from the perspective of a practitioner who has built this movement from the ground up. I believe these valuable nuggets of truth will help you as you consider leading this movement in your congregation. So please take a few minutes and read Dave's words of guidance.

* * *

One thing I've learned about the Take It Home approach is that we must really understand our goals if we want to be successful. Most of the time in the church, we tend to measure success by the impact, intensity, excitement or fun that we or the participants feel during an event. We ask questions such as:

- Were the kids into the singing during Vacation Bible School?
- Did the kids in youth group spend time bonding on their ski trip?
- How much discussion about the Bible lesson took place in the small group?
- Were the men really engaged and listening during the teaching time at their men's ministry meeting?

While these are great questions, they're not the ultimate question. The big question when it comes to faith at home isn't about whether the event was fun, exciting, engaging or filled with passion and energy, but rather, what happens when the families go home from the event? We need to evaluate ourselves on what happens in the *home* as the result of our programs and events.

So instead of asking if parents enjoyed the story, activity or music, we should be asking if they're implementing devotions, prayer or service into their routines at home with their kids. If an event seems pretty average but Dad is now doing devotions with his daughter each night before bedtime, then you've succeeded. If Mom is praying with the kids before breakfast or families are now serving together once a month in the community, score yourself an A+ and take the day off. You deserve it!

How can you get to that point in your faith at home ministry? Let's look at some important principles as you start building the Take It Home events that Mark described in the last chapter.

Upfront Encouragement

> Upfront: Honest; candid; straightforward;
> initial investment; in advance; beforehand;
> direct; forthright; genuine.

If you look up the word "upfront" in a dictionary or thesaurus, you'll find a similar list of words. I would like to use this list to offer some honest, candid, straightforward, forthright, direct, genuine, initial investments you need to know in advance—that is, some important things to keep in mind before you begin to empower families to make their homes a place where faith is nurtured.

Nurture Their Nature

Recently, I was reading a book on understanding yourself that was based on the Myers-Briggs Type Indicator. You probably know that Myers-Briggs is a personality test that identifies a person's individual preferences or characteristics. However, the author of the book I was reading made the staggering point that personality is made up of two components. The first is temperament, a configuration of predisposed inclinations. The second is character, a configuration of learned habits and disciplines. In other words, children are born with a temperament that God gives them—ingrained inclinations that they cannot and would not want to change.

However, parents have an amazing opportunity and responsibility to take the unique temperament of each child and overlay it with the character of God by instilling habits and disciplines that will keep them connected to Christ. Did you catch that? *Parents have the most power and influence over the habits and disciplines formed in their children.* If we as pastors have embraced the faith at home movement, this clearly means that we must empower parents to successfully overlay Christ-connecting habits into the lives of their children. When this happens, children will truly grow up to become all that God desires them to be.

Help Parents See into Future Generations!

We all know from personal experience that much of what we do in our homes is the result of what we grew up with. Dad read the paper every morning at the table while drinking a cup of coffee before work. Why? Because that's what dads do. We open one Christmas gift on Christmas Eve and the rest on Christmas morning. Why? Because that's how our parents did it when we were kids. For Thanksgiving, we eat that green-bean casserole with cream of mushroom soup in it. Why? Because Mom made that dish every year for Thanksgiving.

We could come up with thousands of other examples of how we do things because that's the way they were done in our homes growing up. Often, we don't even realize the reason we do certain things. They have become so much a part of who we are that we just do them without a second thought.

The same will be true of the families in our church. For instance, if the families in your church start praying, blessing their children, doing devotions as a family, spending time in service together or worshiping together on a regular basis, those kids will grow up doing those things themselves *and* teach those disciplines to their own kids. Why? Because it will subconsciously become a part of who they are. "That's what we always did at my house and that's just what families do, isn't it?"

Look at the big picture here. Your little event might not only influence one child or family but may also change entire families and multitudes of people for generations to come! So part of your job is to cast that vision for the parents in your church. Then you can watch them get excited as they realize the power of the opportunity you're placing in their hands.

Disciple Parents Through Their Kids!

How many times have you seen or heard about people who come *back* to church because they now have kids? It's true. Ministry to children provides a wonderful evangelism tool for the Church and ultimately the Kingdom. But all too often churches don't see children as a tool for the discipleship of parents. After the parents are in the doors, we instantly separate them from their children and try to entice them into an adult-specific discipleship program. The problem is that just as parents weren't motivated to come to church before they had kids, they aren't really motivated to come to an extra church program just for them.

So remember that these parents came because of their kids. That's one of the beauties of our Take It Home events. Under the guise of providing something good for their kids and family, we can ultimately teach parents about incorporating spiritual disciplines into not only the lives of their children but their own lives as well.

Take prayer, for example. If we teach about prayer when kids are just seven or eight years old, it's pretty basic stuff. But realistically, that's exactly what most of our parents need. And because "it's for the kids," many adults will personally begin to engage God through prayer for the first time. Add teaching about family worship, devotions, service and Scripture reading before kids even hit their teenage years. If that's not discipleship, I don't know what is!

Culture Change

Culture: The behaviors, beliefs and characteristics
of a particular social, ethnic, or age group
that have been ingrained through training,
experience, perception and practice.

Helping families in your church see that their home is the primary place where faith is nurtured requires a significant shift in their thinking. In fact, it's a total culture shift, because it flies in the face of the behaviors, beliefs and characteristics that have been ingrained in them through training, experience, perception and practice. So how can you help them through this culture change?

Admit It's an Uphill Battle

One thing I love about airports are those moving sidewalks. You can be sauntering along on them, and when you look at others who aren't on the moving sidewalk, you realize that you're really moving fast. Little effort, maximum speed—what a great deal!

Unfortunately, this will *not* be your experience as you work to get families to own responsibility for passing on faith to their children. I wish it was. I wish I could tell you that you could jump into some faith at home stream and the current would sweep you away downriver. I wish I could say, "Just get the ball rolling and things will take care of themselves." Of course, I could tell you all of that, but it would be a lie. The truth is that if you take the call to empower families seriously, you will face an uphill climb. Not only does our society create roadblocks for families, but also during the past 40 years our church culture has assumed the faith-passing responsibility of parents. Changing that mindset won't be easy.

Surprisingly, if you challenge the underlying belief in most families and congregations that church is the place where kids learn about faith in Christ, you won't encounter an out-and-out rebellion. No, it will be worse. You'll encounter passive resistance.

People won't argue with you, throw temper tantrums or speak out against your efforts at church board meetings—they'll just passively not engage. They've been heavily influenced by a culture that teaches them to drop off their children for faith. And that culture is hard to change.

So, from the beginning, be aware that you're fighting years of American culture and church culture. While this might not seem like a big change, it will take some time for the shift to occur.

Be a Broken Record

In order to fight the prevailing culture, families in your church need to hear a consistent and constant message from you that reminds and encourages them as they attempt to go where very few other families and churches have gone before. (Sorry, I love referencing Star Trek!)

Use every opportunity. Will your people get tired of hearing it? I hope so, but it's up to you to send a message! Say it again and again. Tell people in your church that it's up to them, that you can't do it without them, that they have been given an amazing opportunity to instill faith in their kids, and that the church is there to support them and reinforce what happens in their homes. Say it however you like, but say it and say it often.

Imagine Your Church Is from Missouri—Show Them!

One of my buddies is famous for making a statement and then following it up by saying, "That and $5 will buy you a cup of coffee at Starbucks." This not only points out how expensive a cup of coffee at Starbucks is (for the record, it's more like a buck-fifty for plain ol' coffee) but also, more importantly, that we can't just talk about empowering families. We have to *show* people how serious we are.

One way to show your church that faith in the home is a priority is by preaching about it. In most churches, the most influential and important place of communication is the pulpit. So if the topic of an entire sermon is about families living out their faith, people will see the value your church places on what happens in the home. If you make this topic the focus of several sermons, your congregation will really take notice.

Another concrete and practical way to show your congregation that the home is where this faith movement will take place is through the example of how you spend your time. If people hear you talking a lot about the home but see you spending 99 percent of your energy planning church programs for kids, your words and $5 will buy you a cup of coffee at Starbucks! How you spend your time and energy will make a statement to the people of your church—and they will notice!

If you want to spend time and energy on empowering families, something else might need to end. Planning and implementing some of the Take It Home events Mark mentioned in chapter 3 is a great first step. You can also find more practical ideas and resources in *Take It Home*.

Finally, you must demonstrate your commitment to building faith at home through the ways you allocate your church's resources. All churches have limited resources. Often, we have to make tough decisions about how we use those resources to move the Kingdom forward through our ministries. When parents see significant portions of church resources—including staffing—being used to empower what's happening in their homes, it will make a significant statement to them about what you really believe in and the expectations you have of them as parents and families. Investing quality resources in the families of your congregation sends a strong message that they won't forget.

You Say You Want an Evolution?

Evolution: A process of gradual,
peaceful growth and development
resulting in transformation.

As Mark stated in the last chapter, you don't always need to rework your entire ministry. Most likely, what you're currently doing is wonderful ministry for kids. So your goal is to begin the process of gradual, peaceful growth and development that will result in the transformation of families from the inside out.

Not Revolution

I played college basketball at Hastings College, a small private school in Nebraska (go Broncos!). Despite being a small school, we had a lot of basketball tradition. Both our coach and our team took being the best we could be very seriously. After all, we represented Hastings on the court.

For four years, I spent countless hours practicing and working on my game. But even with all the energy and effort I expended, there were times when it seemed I wasn't improving all that much. One day, shortly after my senior season had wrapped up, I played one-on-one with a buddy who I had played against four years earlier. He was at Hastings on a football scholarship. He was a great athlete, and I remembered him being a good basketball player—I had just barely been able to beat him in a game when we were freshmen. Well, this game was a completely different story. I not only beat him, but I also skunked him. He didn't score a single point. After the game ended, he said, "Man, you've really gotten a lot better!" That was when I realized how much all those hours really had improved my game. It wasn't that noticeable along the way, but looking back it was as clear as day.

The same will be true of your ministry to empower families. Three months from now, you won't notice a dramatic difference in the families and children in your church. A Take It Home event isn't a magic formula that creates instantaneous results. If that's what you're looking for, you won't find it there. What you will find is an approach to family ministry that will slowly and almost undetectably transform families from the inside out over the course of many years.

This isn't a magic diet pill that promises to help you fit into your high school prom dress or wedding tux in two weeks. Empowering the home, like anything else worth having, will take hours of work. You have to believe in it. You have to trust that it will work. You have to accept by faith that it is working. But most important, you have to know that it's right!

CHAPTER 4 SUMMARY:

- You have a great opportunity and a great responsibility.

- Change the way the people of your church live their lives at home.

- Set a course that produces results for generations.

- The folly of looking for instantaneous results and quick fixes.

- The wisdom of staying the course.

- Discover the preferred future God wants to accomplish in, through and beyond us.

- A commitment to be a faith at home church needs to outlast the leadership that makes it.

- The tale of the Simpsons.

- People want a way to connect faith with their daily lives.

- What will your legacy be?

- The difficulty of measuring success.

- The importance of choosing your environment wisely.

- The importance of building the right environment.

- The importance of *being* a God-loving, God-following, Christ-in-us environment.

How Do We Commit to This?

Jesus . . . loved fruit. Not the kind you pick off trees or vines, but the
kind that's evident in the life of a person whom He has changed.
He made very clear that the proof of people's faith is not in the information
they know or the religious gathering they attend, but in the way they
integrate what they know and believe into their everyday practices. . . .
The Lord encountered numerous people during His earthly tenure who
could quote Scripture or pretend they knew and loved Him. But His
reaction to them was always the same: "Show me the fruit."[1]

George Barna

Calvary Lutheran in Golden Valley, Minnesota, where I served
as youth and family ministry pastor before coming to Ventura
Missionary Church, made the commitment to be a church *of*
family ministry more than 20 years ago. I remember seeing
firsthand the results of this long-term commitment in a not
so normal dynamic that took place in the junior high ministry.

Calvary had a large-group/small-group oriented junior
high ministry. This meant that we needed more than 60 adult
small-group leaders who each met with a group of 6 to 8 students every Wednesday evening. Obviously, in a normal church
situation, finding 60 adults willing to spend 2 hours every
Wednesday evening with a small group of squirrely junior high
students is typically a difficult task. Yet we didn't have a problem at all at Calvary. In fact, most years we had more adults

willing to serve than we had openings! How did this happen?

As students registered for the program, we asked them to list the names of two students with whom they would like to be in a small group as well as one adult they would like as their small-group leader (the adult name was optional). I'll never forget the first year I saw the number of names turned in and who the names were. The people most requested for small-group leaders were the students' parents!

As I thought about how counter to our culture this seemed, I realized what was different at Calvary. From the day a child was born, the church lived by its commitment to train the parents through Take It Home events. This included how to bless their children when they were infants, how to pray with the kids when they were four-year-olds, how to do devotions with them as first-graders, how to read the Bible with them as third-graders, and how to do service projects as an action of faith with them as fifth-graders. Thanks to this long-term partnership, by the time these kids moved into the junior high program, it was no big deal for them to ask their parents to join them as small-group leaders in the next step of their faith journey.

This truly is counter cultural! But this environment didn't come about in 40 days—it was the result of 20 years of commitment.

Great Opportunity, Great Responsibility

As you ponder what this kind of long-term commitment could mean for your own church, let's review the journey we've taken to this point. We've taken a critical look at what we're accomplishing (or, more accurately, not accomplishing) through the program-driven approach to ministry that has prevailed in churches over the past three to four decades. We've concluded that despite the fact that the church today is offering some of the best programs ever offered in and through the church, godly living—personified by prayer, Bible reading, devotions and faith talk—isn't taking place in homes today. Further, the Church has unintentionally enabled this to happen. Worse, unless something changes, people will continue to be engaged in church programs yet disengaged in their faith walk at home. This eventually results in overall disengagement.

As pastors and church leaders, we must ask ourselves if we want to enable this same pattern to continue or if we're willing to make some changes that will help families bring Christ back into the center of their homes. Now is our time to lead the Church. The personal decisions we make today will influence generations to come. This is both a great opportunity as well as a great responsibility. And let's be honest—it's certainly not for the weak of heart, because it does require a long-term commitment.

Perhaps another way to look at this commitment is to think about how you would like to be remembered 30 years from now. Is your goal for just 10 percent of the people of your church to be praying, reading the Bible or engaging in faith talk in their homes? Or would you like someone to tell a story like the one I told about Calvary Lutheran's junior highers?

A Fresh View

Thankfully, if you're willing to make this kind of long-term commitment, you don't need to overhaul everything you do or launch some expensive new program. The solution is found in putting on that faith at home set of lenses that will help you see and shape your ministry in a new way. This fresh and clear view will change the way the people of your church live their lives at home, which will then spill over into how they live at work, in their communities and in the world!

Over time, through Take It Home events and other adaptations you make, the focus among the people in your congregation will become more about what happens at home than what happens at church. Faith at home will become a critical string woven through your mission, vision and strategy. This string will subtly, yet strategically, transform your church's ministry to bring Christ and Christlike living back into the center of every home.

The current family crisis didn't happen overnight. So it makes sense that the work we need to do to restore families won't happen quickly or easily either. Yet we desperately need to make a renewed commitment to faith at home. If we don't start now, we'll simply be enabling the same behaviors to continue in churches and families and only compound the problem.

Researcher George Barna confirms this: "Unfortunately, as far as we can determine, the family will remain a mere blip on the radar screen when it comes to serving as the conduit for faith experience and expression, remaining central to perhaps 5 percent of the population."[2] I don't know about you, but I'm not satisfied with just 5 percent of families having Christ in the center of their homes. And I'm quite certain that Christ isn't satisfied with it either. Therefore, it's time for the Church to rise up and make a new commitment to family ministry. If we don't, nothing will truly change.

Reinstilling faith at home won't happen overnight. But if you make a commitment today, you'll be setting a course that has the opportunity to produce results for generations to come.

"I Want It Now!"

Let's be blunt: In all likelihood, becoming a faith at home-driven church will not produce instantaneous results and growth. Considering the culture we live in, I realize this isn't a good selling point, but I want to be completely honest with you. Becoming a faith at home-driven church probably will not make the Top 10 list of ideas for church growth. So if you're looking for a quick way to boost attendance or see your church budget increase, building faith at home isn't what you're looking for.

One thing that continually amazes me about our culture is how quick-fix-oriented we've become. We want instant gratification. If a professional sports coach doesn't lead his team to a championship within a few years, he gets fired. A recent commercial I saw boldly proclaimed through a very annoying hard-rock jingle, "I want it all! I want it all! I want it now!" We eat fast food, drive fast cars, have the fastest computers with the fastest Internet connection, and we attempt to lose weight as fast as we can by drinking Slim Fast! Often, our culture determines the success of a program or product solely by the amount of time it takes to produce results.

Remember the TV show *Seinfeld* from a few years back? In one of my favorite episodes, Kramer walks into Jerry's apartment with his latest million-dollar idea and says, "Jerry, you've heard of the 10-minute abs video that promises you great abs in 10 minutes, haven't you?"

"Yes, I have," Jerry replies.

Kramer then excitedly announces, "I'm coming out with a new video that's going to make me rich. It's called 9-minute abs. You can't tell me that if my 9-minute abs video is sitting on the shelf next to their 10-minute abs video that everyone won't buy mine."

Jerry then responds, "That makes sense, Kramer. But I have one question for you. What if someone comes out with an 8-minute abs video?"

Kramer, stunned and totally taken aback by the thought, simply responds, "No one would do that. Everyone knows you can't get great abs in 8 minutes!"

As funny and ridiculous as that episode was, it illustrates what our culture has become. If we can achieve results faster, we'll go for it.

In many ways, as pastors we get caught up in this same reality and feel the same pressure. If we don't produce instantaneous results—measured typically by increased attendance, new
programs, better giving and building programs—then we feel
that we might need to consider a new calling. There's always
another church that is growing faster, preaching better and
being more creative and innovative than we are. If our church
isn't bursting at the seams and hitting record numbers every
year, we can easily feel that we're failing.

Instead of focusing on where the Lord uniquely calls us to go
as a church, we look across the street or halfway around the world
at another church and say, "That's what we need to do here!" The
chase continues to find the next innovative program or dynamic
staff person who can provide that quick fix and instantaneous
result we feel pressured to accomplish. As church consultant
Thom Rainer writes, "Churches and their lay leaders can be
incredibly demanding of, if not vicious to, pastors. In my con-
sulting ministry with the Rainer Group, I often deal with lay
leaders who treat pastors like CEOs and expect immediate
results of them."[3]

Long-Term Versus Quick Fix

About four years into my ministry as senior pastor of Ventura
Missionary Church, I had to face this reality at a board and
staff retreat. Let me provide a little background information so
that you can better understand what was taking place.

VMC experienced exponential growth in the 1980s and early
1990s as the church grew from 80 people to more than 1,500. At
the same time, the city of Ventura grew from roughly 40,000
people to more than 100,000. When I arrived, the church had
been on a 3-year decline, with some 850 people attending worship services. Due to some strong anti-growth campaigns that

undermined new housing development plans, the city of Ventura had also stopped growing. In spite of this, the church had a strong desire to grow and reach the lost for Christ.

As a young and naïve pastor, I was excited to be a part of a church that wanted to grow. I believed we could easily turn the ship around and become a growing congregation again. However, this turned out to be a much more difficult task than I had realized.

During the first two years, we were able to stop the downward spiral and grow to more than 1,000. But then we plateaued for the next two years. During this plateau time, we became more committed to our faith at home focus and initiated many of our Take It Home events. In the first years of this new vision, as is often the case, the Take It Home events were works in progress. Still, families began to experience for the first time the opportunity to pray, read the Bible, lead devotions, bless their children and do family service projects together. We started to hear stories of how moms and dads were doing these ideas at home.

As the climate at VMC began to change, each ministry took more ownership in the faith at home vision we established. In just a six-month period of time, we even had two of the largest baptism classes that the church had ever held. Many of the people who came to be baptized included children and their parents who were part of our faith at home focus.

Taking Action

However, in spite of these successes, our overall attendance numbers weren't increasing. This created significant concern for some of our leadership, including me. So I pulled away the pastoral staff for a two-day retreat to openly discuss the state of VMC. A very instrumental book that we used during our time together was *Breakout Churches* by Thom Rainer. In this book,

Rainer, a church consultant, told the story of 13 churches that had experienced a time of plateau and then, under the same leadership, had seen a time of sustained growth.

During this pastoral staff retreat, I wanted all of the members to put their cards on the table and give me their honest feedback of where we were as a church. So I asked them the following questions that we then discussed:

- Is VMC healthy?
- Why isn't VMC growing?
- Do we need to change anything?
- Is my preaching a problem?
- Does the church's vision need to change?

When the retreat ended, I couldn't believe where God had led us in such a short amount of time. The overwhelming consensus of the team was to simply stay the course! If anything, the pastoral team calmed me down and helped me to see that the faith at home changes that we were in the process of making needed more time to develop. The staff was excited and committed about the fruit we were already seeing. While I felt the pressure to see numeric growth, they were more excited to see us become the church we were in the process of becoming!

Through the pastoral staff, God lifted my eyes to look past the immediate results. He caused me to refocus my attention on the long-term commitment we had made to be a church of small groups and missional living as well as a faith at home-driven church.

Spreading the Message

After the staff retreat, I felt reinvigorated. I yearned to have the church's general board arrive at the same conclusion that the pastoral team had arrived at. So I invited the general board to a daylong retreat with the pastors.

It was at this retreat that I came face to face with the truth that not everyone saw things from the same long-term perspective as the staff and I did. Toward the end of the retreat, one of the general board members asked the group a very difficult set of questions: "Are we sure we're on the right course? When we called Pastor Mark, I was under the impression from him and others that we would experience growth. Yet we aren't growing. I hate to ask this, but I wonder if we need to ask ourselves if we're sure we have the right leader? Are we headed in the right direction?"

At that point, you could have heard a pin drop in the room. I realized that everyone was looking at me. In that defining moment, God gave me an extra measure of peace (thanks to the previous retreat with the pastoral staff). God also gave me an answer that I didn't see coming.

It went something like this: "I can understand and appreciate what you're saying. To be honest, I've asked that same question of myself, and I'm partly responsible for the questions you have. When I came to VMC, I definitely painted a picture of growth that I thought would take place during the first few years. As I look back on things now, if I could change anything, that's what I would change. I had no idea then how long it would take to make the changes we need to make to become the church I believe God wants us to become. Since then, I've learned that becoming a church *of* small groups takes time. Becoming a missional church takes time. And becoming a church *of* faith at home takes time. I've come to realize that none of these changes are quick fixes. Yet I still believe with all my heart that these are the right things for VMC to become. They simply take longer than I thought they would."

Then, summoning all the courage I could, I issued a challenge: "So now I have some questions for you. Do you still believe that being a church *of* small groups is of God and the right direction to go? Do you still believe that being a missional church is of God and the right direction to go? Do you still believe that being a church *of* faith at home is of God and the right direction to go? If so, we need to stay the course and be patient. The fruit—like we're already beginning to see through the numbers of people being baptized—will continue to come."

You might think that the questions raised by this general board member created dissension or disharmony among us. But it did just the opposite. The questions challenged all of us to look at the importance of what we were doing. Were we going to be a quick-fix-oriented church? Or did God have something greater that He wanted us to accomplish? Were we really committed to the faith at home vision long term? Personally, was I willing to stand up for becoming this kind of church even if it didn't produce instantaneous growth?

At that point, God began growing me to think beyond the next few months to see the future He wanted us to accomplish.

Integral and Organic

I'm sharing this experience because I want you to know that I understand the pressure you face as a pastor or church leader to produce results quickly. Unfortunately, this pressure produces short-term thinking, which I'm not sure is the best thing for the Church. Instead, you need to look beyond yourself to see the preferred future that God wants to accomplish in, through and beyond you. *Then you need to roll up your sleeves and do the arduous work it takes to lead your church in the direction it needs to go, no matter how long it takes or how much resistance you face.*

Thom Rainer confirms this in *Breakout Churches* when he writes, "Most of the breakout churches in our study did not experience explosive overnight growth. For most, the path of growth was slow, methodical, and strewn with obstacles. Persistent, never-say-die leadership was a key instrument that God used to grow these churches to the next level. Giving up was always a temptation but never an option."[4]

If you're looking for a quick fix to transform families and bring Christ back into the center of every home, you're not going to find it. If any program you can purchase is offering such a quick fix, beware! The disintegration of the family has been evolving for generations, so I believe it's foolish to think we can fix it with a 40-day program or a weekend retreat. Satan has intentionally and methodically taken Christ out of the home over the past several generations. Barring God's miraculous intervention, it will take generations to firmly establish Christ at the center of every home again.

Therefore, I'm convinced that each church must make a long-term commitment to becoming a faith at home-driven church. This commitment will need to outlast you and the current leadership of your church. It will need to become an integral and organic part of your church and how you do church. (More on this later.)

Long-Term Impact

Before I forget, let me complete the story of what happened at our staff and general board retreats. The difficult question the board member asked forced us to examine ourselves. We realized that we needed to determine God's unique purpose both for VMC and for me as pastor. Seeking God's will and purpose is *never* a bad thing. I praise God for the general board member who took a risk when he asked some difficult questions that needed to be asked.

In the weeks that followed, the pastoral staff and general board recommitted to staying the course with the vision God had given VMC. I became even more committed and felt an inner peace that I had never sensed before. Sometimes, difficult questions provide exactly what we need!

I've led, and on occasion will probably continue to lead, the 40-day programs known for attracting new people to churches. While these programs and sermon series have their purpose, I think we need to be careful not to get caught in the trap of going from one flashy program to another. By themselves, these programs focus largely on numbers and instantaneous results instead of looking at the long-term impact our ministry is making.

The latest "dancing elephant" program might draw new spectators for a period of time, but will it truly impact and equip people to make the necessary changes for them to be stronger spiritually 10 or 15 years from now? *What matters most to me is not getting more people into our church buildings or programs but getting Jesus into the homes of the people who come to our church buildings and programs!*

Does this mean your church won't grow if it becomes a faith at home-driven church? Absolutely not. I simply mean that it probably won't produce *instantaneous* growth. The fruit will come, but it might be 5, 10, 25, 50 or even 100 years down the road.

The Simpsons—Not Homer and Bart

When your church makes the commitment to help individuals and families be healthier and stronger at home, you won't be able to keep people away who want the same thing in their life. Annette Simpson, who two years ago started attending VMC with her husband, Jim, excitedly shared the following story with me:

> Pastor Mark, we just had to meet with you to share our experience with you and to tell you about the impact your faith at home emphasis has made in our lives.

For more than 20 years, we attended a mainline church in the community. Week after week, we went to church and simply put in our time going through the motions. The music was nice and the messages were fine. Yet when we went home, that was pretty much the end of our time with God.

When we came to your church, we were continually confronted with the challenge to continue at home the faith experience we were having at church. I'll never forget the Sunday afternoon when my husband said, "Maybe we should try praying or reading the Bible together like Pastor Mark says."

After I picked up my jaw off the floor, we decided that we'd begin praying together each day and that we'd read the Bible together two times a week. I have to be honest—it wasn't easy at first. But we've gotten more used to it, and it has completely changed our home life.

My only regret is that I wish we could have come to your church sooner! I've thought to myself, *Where was this emphasis when we were raising our children? Maybe things would have turned out differently.*

Our grown kids now have children of their own, but unfortunately they spent many years not following the Lord or attending church. As I look back now, that's probably a result of the way we treated religion. It was something we simply did or made our kids do on Sunday mornings.

When Jim and I shared with our children that we'd started attending a new church and that we are now praying and reading the Bible together, we were very surprised at how interested they were. They immediately asked what church we were going to. When we told them—again to our surprise—they asked if they could go to church with us some Sunday!

On the first Sunday they came, you gave an "as for me and my household, we will serve the Lord" challenge. Our adult children, who are now parents themselves, went forward and picked up a rock indicating that they want to be faith at home families! They now attend church with us every week and want to have our grandchildren dedicated!

I can't thank you enough, because we now get to come alongside our children and help them do something we didn't do ourselves. I guess this change didn't come too late after all!

This is just one example of what can happen when you make the long-term commitment to being a faith at home church. Many people simply don't live out faith at home because they haven't been challenged, inspired and equipped to do so. And while a faith at home emphasis might not produce instantaneous growth, we need to recognize that the impact of faith at home will last for generations!

The Simpson family was forever changed the day they started to pray and read the Bible in the home. What an awesome realization! And this change has affected their children and children's children who will follow in their footsteps. Imagine what life will be like for the Simpsons' grandchildren who will grow up in a home filled with faith talk, prayer, Bible reading and Jesus in the center of everything they do. If you think that's good, what will life be like for the generation that follows?

God Versus Religion

You might have noticed that the Simpsons didn't need to do a lot of convincing to get their children re-engaged in their faith walk. All Annette and Jim had to do was talk about the way the church had helped them and their adult children were interested immediately.

Most people today are exceedingly open and interested in God, Jesus, spirituality and holy living. Many surveys reveal that most people claim they believe in God. Yet when I personally visit with unchurched people, I frequently hear that the reason they don't attend church is because organized religion has become all about programs, buildings and numbers.

Sadly, people today associate Christian faith with organized religion and church activities when all they're really searching for is a way to connect faith with their daily lives. When people hear that a place exists that can help them bring faith and godly living into their homes, they're open and excited to give it a try, even if it means giving church another chance.

At VMC, we have a radio ministry. Our annual contract provides the opportunity to create a 60-second radio spot that gets played 200 times per month on 3 different secular radio stations. This ministry offers us the opportunity to keep Christ and the church on the radar for the unchurched people in our communities.

Instead of promoting programs at our church, we use these ads to speak truth into our community. Our goal is to dispel some existing stereotypes and open doors for people to give God another chance. The following is the script of one radio ad we aired:

Hello, this is Pastor Mark of Ventura Missionary Church, and I want to begin by apologizing to you on behalf of the Christian Church. Unfortunately, over the last 40 to 50 years, we've become very program and building focused. Many churches have moved away from focusing on what's happening in the home to what's happening at church. As a result, most people today—including many church-goers—have no idea how to live a godly lifestyle at home.

At Ventura Missionary Church, we've made a significant change to become a faith at home-driven church. We've decided that what matters to us most is not what happens at church but what happens at home. Yes, we still have programs. But every program we offer is designed to help you bring godly living home so that you and your family will be blessed.

If this interests you, I invite you to give God another chance and begin your journey of bringing faith home by coming to one of our three Sunday services at 8:00, 9:30 or 11:00. To find Ventura Missionary Church, simply take Victoria north to Foothill, turn right and VMC will be about a mile ahead on your left.

See you this Sunday! God bless.

This radio spot created a variety of different responses. On one hand, some fellow local pastors weren't too happy with me for pointing out the building and program focus that many churches have. On the other hand, many of the unchurched in our community responded favorably, which made it all worth it. We received more positive emails and had more visitors because of this one ad than many of the previous radio spots we had done.

A Legacy Mindset

Are you able to get your arms around the point that I'm trying to make? If you decide to make a long-term commitment to leading a faith at home church, chances are you won't see instantaneous growth. Yet this commitment will affect your church and the people God brings there for generations!

A faith at home commitment will outlast any building you build or program you lead. Instead of having your name attached to a building project you instigated, wouldn't you rather see Christ's name on the doorframes of every house in your community? What an exciting prospect! Christlike living will continue in the homes and families of your community long after buildings have been demolished. Yet this can only happen if churches make a long-term commitment to establish a model of family ministry that will train and equip families to bring Christ into their homes.

Thom Rainer writes that one of the key distinguishing marks of a breakout leader is "the desire to see the church do well and to make a difference well beyond the ministry of the current leadership."[5] He goes on to list comments of several of these leaders, who have what Rainer describes as a "legacy perspective":

- "I pray that God will allow me to look at this church from heaven 50 years from now and find out that the fruit of what we did is lasting."

- "Every time we look at doing something new or making some change, we ask how this might affect the church 25 years from now."

- "Some of the ideas we have may be quick fixes. We are asking God what will work for the long haul."

- "I pray that the church I leave one day will be a better church for my successor."[6]

Rainer concludes, "The ambition and drive of these leaders cannot be denied. And that ambition is not limited to their personal successes. They are ambitious for the church to be thriving and healthy well beyond their ministries and even their lifetimes."[7]

As pastors and church leaders, we need to ask ourselves if we are willing to look beyond the quick fix and near future to a long-term goal with long-term impact. We need to consider if we are willing to stay the course and lead the faith at home movement forward even when resistance comes.

We need to realize that we're in a battle with Satan. This battle is being waged in each and every family. Satan won't simply give up and give back the home easily. Therefore, making a long-term faith at home commitment will challenge our church and us because it's not as easy to understand or evaluate as launching another quick-fix program.

Again, Rainer is blunt about the challenges: "The breakout churches showed us that the path was neither simple nor easy. And perhaps that is one key reason so few church leaders decide to pay the price to lead their churches to greatness."[8] Are you willing to pay the price? Are you willing to make a long-term commitment to becoming a faith at home church "so that you, your children and their children after them may fear the Lord your God as long as you live by keeping all his decrees and commands that I give you, and so that you may enjoy long life" (Deut. 6:2)?

Defining Success

As a pastor, I can't imagine anything better than seeing Christ affect the way people live their lives at home. I get so excited knowing that the transformation occurring in the home affects not just those individuals but also their family for generations as well!

As great as this is, one of the most difficult realities you will face is the fact that it's not easy to measure the success of being a faith at home church. You can easily measure if a "40 Days of Purpose" program is successful based on attendance and the number of small groups you have. You can measure the success of your small-group ministry through the percentage of people engaged in some sort of small group. You can even measure the success of your worship services based on attendance. But how do you measure the success of faith at home?

When I asked this question at one of our staff meetings, Bob DuPar, our small-groups pastor, gave me a great answer: "We need to be continually asking ourselves the question, 'Is this transferable?' Is what we're doing at VMC transferring into how people live at home?"

I recognize that measuring the success of faith at home is much more difficult than measuring attendance or giving. Yet "more difficult" certainly doesn't mean that we shouldn't do it. In fact, while it's easy to measure attendance and giving, maybe we've been measuring the wrong things—especially when we're confronted with the truth that the godly living we teach about in our programs isn't transferring into the way people live their lives at home. In other words, our numbers and finances might look great, but if godly living, spiritual growth, discipleship or whatever we want to call it isn't transferring into changed behavior at home, are we truly being successful? I like how researcher George Barna puts it:

> One of the most important lessons I've learned from studying the words of Jesus is that He loved fruit. Not the kind you pick off trees or vines, but the kind that's evident in the life of a person whom He has changed. He made very clear that the proof of people's faith is not in the information they know or the religious gathering they attend, but in the way they integrate what they know and believe into their everyday practices. The hallmarks of the Church that Jesus died for are clear, based on Scripture: your profession of faith in Christ must be supported by a lifestyle that provides irrefutable evidence of your complete devotion to Jesus. The Lord encountered numerous people during His earthly tenure who could quote Scripture or pretend they knew and loved Him. But His reaction to them was always the same: "Show me the fruit." Jesus did not die on the cross to fill church auditoriums, to enable

magnificent church campuses to be funded, or to motivate people to implement innovative programs. He died
because he loves you and me, He wants an everlasting
relationship with us, and he expects that connection
to be so all-consuming that we become wholly transformed—Jesus clones, if you will indulge the expression.[9]

At Ventura Missionary Church, our mission is to introduce
people to a growing relationship with Jesus Christ. When people
ask if our mission statement means that we're a seeker-oriented
church or a build-the-believer-focused church, we simply reply,
"Yes!" Actually, we don't engage in the argument. Instead, we
say that we're a "growing relationship" church.

For us, this means that we want everyone (including lost people) to have a growing, ever-evolving, life-changing relationship
that is deep, close and personal with the one true God of the uni-
verse, through His son Jesus Christ! Obviously, you can't have a
relationship with someone you don't spend time with or invite
into your daily life. Anyone who has been married can attest to
the fact that you don't really know someone until you've lived
with that person over a period of time. In the same way, you
can't have a relationship with Jesus until you live together.

Therefore, at VMC we define success as seeing more people
inviting Christ into the center of their lives at home in order to
enter into a growing relationship with him. Numeric growth still
matters to us, but it's just one side of the coin. Equally important
is the environment we're helping to create in the home.

Long-Term Environment

Writing a book like this takes a significant amount of time,
which is a rare commodity for a senior pastor, husband and
father. I set aside a few extra days to write this chapter while

attending a pastor's conference in Orlando, Florida. I arrived on Friday and began working on this chapter on Saturday. On Sunday morning, I went to Northland Community Church and had the privilege of listening to a message given by senior pastor Dr. Joel Hunter. I had never attended Northland Community Church, nor had I ever heard Dr. Hunter preach before. Yet the message he gave that Sunday morning serves as the perfect, God-given conclusion to this chapter.

Each point Dr. Hunter made in his message ties into the journey we've taken in this chapter. So, with his permission, I'm going to use my recollections and notes of the message as a way to close this chapter. I'm also adding a few application questions to each section for you to consider as well. (I love how God works! He took me to Orlando to hear a pastor's message that He wanted me to share with you as the concluding thoughts and challenges of this chapter. God never ceases to amaze me!)

Dr. Hunter's sermon, based on Genesis 1:18-25, was titled, "God, Executive Producer: The Narrative of Creation." Dr. Hunter began the message by discussing how God made the expanse of air so that birds could fly in the "open expanse of the heavens." He made the expanse of the sea for the "great sea monsters and every other living creature that moves, with which the waters swarmed after their kind." And God made the expanse of the ground for the "cattle and creeping things and beasts of the earth after their kind." In fact, God created these environments so that each kind of animal could live life to the fullest.

Dr. Hunter then explained what God meant when He gave us "dominion." He defined "dominion" as "lording over and protecting others in a way to get the most out of them." Therefore, because we have dominion over the earth, God calls us to protect and serve the environments He created so that the creatures that reside within each one can become everything God created them to be.

1. What's the condition of the home environments of the people in your church?

2. Are these home environments helping people be who God created them to be?

3. As a pastor, are you protecting and serving these home environments?

4. Is the church you lead protecting and serving these home environments?

Dr. Hunter then went on to define three creation principles. The first is the "you choose your environment" principle. Dr. Hunter explained that environment has everything to do with who you'll become, so you need to choose your environment wisely. If you choose a destructive environment, you'll become a destructive person. If you choose a healthy environment, you'll become a healthy person. You become what you behold.

1. What's the state of the home environments of the people of your church—destructive or healthy?

2. In what positive ways do you see your church environment reflected in these home environments?

3. In what negative ways do you see your church environment reflected in these home environments?

The second creation principle is the "you build your environment" principle. Each of us has the ability to build our own environments. So if you want your child, spouse, employee and so forth to develop into a certain kind of person, you need to build the right environment for him or her to grow in. Dr. Hunter cited Starbucks as an example of a business that created an environment for people—and as a result people line up daily all around the world to pay nearly $2 for a cup of coffee!

For us, the good news with this principle is knowing that we can build a faith at home environment. And if we build this environment, the families in our churches—no matter what shape or size—will be able to grow into the people God intended them to be.

---

1. What's the current environment you've built in your church?

2. How does this environment support or take away from faith at home?

3. What environment would you like to build for your faith at home focus?

The final creation principle Dr. Hunter listed is the "you are somebody's environment" principle. With this principle, the challenge is to consider the type of environment you are in the life of those around you. Each of us is an environment to others. So the question becomes: Do we offer a God-loving, God-following, Christ-in-us environment for those we love around us?

1. Who are you an environment to?

2. Who was an environment in your life?

3. What kind of environment are you?

4. What kind of environment would you like to be?

My Own Application

When I wrote my first book, *Faith Begins at Home,* I specifically wanted to inspire, motivate and equip parents to be the primary influencers of faith in the lives of their children. I provided as many practical ideas as I could to help them establish their home as the primary environment where faith would be nurtured. Therefore, I couldn't agree more with Dr. Hunter's final principle.

As pastors and church leaders, we must realize that the people of our churches are looking at the type of environment we're creating in our own homes. One of the greatest compliments I receive is when the leadership of my church affirms my commitment to faith at home—which they've done at every evaluation I've had to date—through the way I clearly value my family and make time for them.

I love the Church, but not at the expense of my family. After my relationship with Jesus Christ comes my relationship with my wife and daughter—and then my commitment to the Church. I'm an environment to my family that can either help influence them to be closer to the Lord or push them farther away.

It's my goal to be an environment that can claim, "*As for me and my household, we will serve the Lord*" (Josh. 24:15, emphasis added).

CHAPTER 5 SUMMARY:

- The senior pastor has a critical role in returning Christ to the center of every home.

- Why leading the faith at home movement requires confident humility.

- What to do if your senior pastor doesn't recognize the need to be faith at home driven.

- Making faith at home an integral part of your church's mission.

- How having a clear faith at home vision can ignite your congregation.

- The importance of committing resources to equip families as faith-nurturers.

- Staffing your faith at home-driven church.

- Avoiding isolated leaders and areas of ministry.

- Elevating faith at home to being a part of how you do church.

- How to get all of your ministries to commit to becoming a church of family ministry.

- Making sure your set of faith at home lenses influences your preaching and teaching?

Will We Be Movement Makers or Movement Breakers?

A mark of leaders, an attribute that puts them in a position to show the way for others, is that they are better than most at pointing the direction. As long as one is leading, one always has a goal. It may be a goal arrived at by group consensus, or the leader, acting on inspiration, may simply have said, "Let's go this way." But the leader always knows what it is and can articulate it for any who are unsure. By clearly stating and restating the goal the leader gives certainty to others who may have difficulty in achieving it for themselves. [1]

Robert Greenleaf

Over the years, I've had the opportunity to lead faith at home movements in the churches where I've served as a youth and family pastor. I've also had the privilege to work with pastors who've led this movement in churches all across the world. I've had the opportunity to see things that can help and hinder a faith at home movement. I call these help/hinder qualities "movement makers or breakers."

In the following sections, I am going to share some of the movement makers and breakers that I've experienced through the years and make some observations about them. Please note that because the faith at home movement is a work in progress, this certainly isn't an exhaustive list. However, I also urge you not to minimize the importance of these movement makers or breakers—

understanding these qualities will be critically important to the success of the faith at home movement in your congregation.

1. The Critical Role of the Senior Pastor

On Thanksgiving eve of 2004, I received a phone call that I knew would come but wasn't prepared for at all. My mom called me from the hospital back in Minneapolis. Through her tears, she said, "Your dad has quit breathing. What do I do?"

My dad had a chronic heart and lung disease, and it was now his time to be with the Lord. I knew my dad's wishes, so I simply and gently said to my mom, "It's okay, Mom. Let him go. Let him go." The next few months were a very difficult time for me, as I had lost not only my father but also my number one mentor and friend. Without my dad to turn to, I often felt as if I were swimming upstream alone as a senior pastor.

This traumatic and grief-filled time came just two years after I had accepted the call to become senior pastor of Ventura Missionary Church. To be completely honest, after my first two years I was burning out trying to be the pastor everyone else wanted me to be, and many people in the church were getting frustrated trying to follow my all-over-the-place leadership. Not only was this my first position as a senior pastor, but I was also following a great pastor who had grown the church from 50 people to more than 1,500 worshipers during his 25 years of leadership. In many cases, the person who follows a very successful, long-term pastor becomes an unintentional interim pastor.

It definitely had been a crazy two years. We were doing a lot. In that short time, we had developed a new mission, vision and strategy; held some seeker-oriented sermon series; worked through the 40 Days of Purpose as a church; launched a small-group ministry; hosted a missional living conference; initiated a new prayer ministry; and completely restructured our children, youth and family ministry program around our new faith at home vision. Yet we weren't settled as a body, and while I wouldn't admit it publicly at the time, I was struggling to hold it all together. Looking back, I can now see that my dad's death magnified the doubts I was having about my ministry.

In late January of the following year—just a few months after my dad died—it was time for my annual review. The review team lovingly shared some things that were very hard for me to hear. I wasn't doing any single specific thing wrong, but the evaluation showed that things at church and within my leadership team were unsettled and needed to improve. Of course, while this was hard to hear, in my heart I knew the evaluation was right on. Again, I had already been sensing that I was burning out, and I was struggling to hold things together.

Interestingly, instead of simply presenting me a list of things I needed to change, the evaluation team asked me one question: "What do you want to do?" That simple question opened the floodgates for a response that—I later realized—I had bottled up for too long.

The words poured out of my mouth and my heart as I released everything I had been holding in: "If I'm going to go down as the senior pastor here, I would rather go down swinging with everything I've got on becoming a church committed to bringing Christ back into the center of every home! My heart breaks when I see what Satan is doing to families. We have to do something about it. I believe the Church is an ocean liner riding across the ocean with the strength to stay afloat through the storms that hit. Each family is a smaller boat. From what I see, the storms are getting bigger, and the majority of these little family boats are taking a beating. Many are sinking fast. If I could do what I wanted, I would deploy *all* of our resources to rescue families of every shape and size.

"If it's a single person living in a nursing home, I want that person to have Christ in the center of his or her nursing home room. I don't care what form of family it is; each family in our church needs

Christ at the center of their home. If we only deploy one line, it won't be enough to rescue them. We have to give it everything we've got so that we can bring our families back up to the surface where they can be restored and float and sail forward again."

When I finished speaking, it felt as if the biggest weight—perhaps the anchor of an ocean liner—had been lifted from my heart and soul. But then I realized that I had vented all of this on the church's elders and my review committee!

I'll never forget their response. "Mark, that's why we called you here. If that's what God has put on your heart, then we want you to go for it! Your team and leaders will support you." From that point on, faith at home became my number one priority—the target on the wall that all of the ministries in our church became focused on.

This became a defining moment for me as a leader. On the very next Sunday, I stood before the congregation and boldly proclaimed our faith at home commitment. The result was an overwhelming spirit of support from the congregation. We soon began to evaluate everything we did as a church through our faith at home lenses. We agreed that our success as a church would not be wrapped up in buildings, programs or numbers but in the impact the ministry had on bringing Christ and Christlike living into the home.

No Resistance

Many movements create disharmony or tension in a church through which a pastor must carefully navigate. This is true when churches start a small-group ministry, change to a contemporary or postmodern style of worship, or aim to become more seeker-friendly. Yet the movement to become a faith at home-driven church is completely different.

When I decided to lead the movement to become a church *of* family ministry at VMC, I anticipated resistance similar to that I had encountered when I led churches through some of the other movements. To my surprise, that resistance never came! Why? Because everyone in the congregation realized that families are struggling and in need of help. The older members had seen the disintegration of families happen during their lifetimes and wanted to see families restored. Younger members immediately committed to it because they knew they would directly benefit from this commitment.

If anything, as I took some bold steps to lead the faith at home movement forward at VMC, the people of the church became more passionate, excited and engaged about where God was leading us. I even felt support from some of the people who had previously been on the sidelines. As a result, I became more energized as well.

Confident Humility

In his research for *Breakout Churches*, Thom Rainer discovered that pastors who were able to successfully lead a breakout movement in their previously plateaued churches shared one key quality and character trait. He summed it up in two words: "confident humility."[2]

It took me a while to sink my teeth into that one, because you don't usually see those two words together. For me, confident humility means that senior pastors who want to lead a faith at home movement must do so in the full confidence that it is of God and that it is exactly what God desires of them. I have complete confidence that Christ wants to reside in the center of every home, and I believe His heart breaks over the fact that most Christians who attend our churches aren't engaged in Christlike living at home.

Those are key words: *confident humility*. Knowing that the present state of families is not how God intended them to be makes me *confident* that I can boldly proclaim that I lead a faith at home-driven church. At the same time, I stand in complete *humility,* humbled by the daunting task of trying to reestablish Christ and Christlike living in the center of every home. Leading a faith at home movement definitely is daunting. It won't be easy. To be honest, it's somewhat overwhelming. Faith at home isn't something we can fix quickly or measure easily. Yet that's even more motivation to come humbly before the Lord to seek His face, strength and ability to do something we can't do ourselves.

I believe that leading a movement to become a church *of* family ministry requires the leadership of a church's senior pastor. While the movement can begin without the senior pastor's initial support (as you'll hear more about from Pastor Dave Teixeira in a bit), at some point the senior pastor of a church must embrace this movement and put on a set of faith at home lenses.

Why is this so important? The senior pastor, along with the primary leadership team of the church, largely determines the direction the church will go and makes many of the staffing, teaching, budget and overall vision decisions. If faith at home isn't on the radar of the senior pastor—or, more important, in the senior pastor's heart—it will be very difficult to make the changes necessary to become a church *of* family ministry.

The Battle for Attention

I'm being honest about these struggles because I want you to know that I fully appreciate and understand the difficult calling that senior pastors have. Everyone wants the senior pastor to champion his or her cause—and the senior pastors are told that if they don't, the ministry won't bear the fruit God intends.

I've been sent on that guilt trip many times. I've even been blamed for the lack of success of some program simply because I didn't make an appropriately passionate announcement about it on Sunday morning. If I respond by pointing out that a lot of churches have thriving programs without a pulpit announcement, somehow my response gets me into even more trouble! But I digress. As you can see, I also know what it feels like to have someone come and say, "In order for this to succeed, you need to support it as the senior pastor."

Pastor to pastor, I'm appealing to you—from your position as the called and appointed leader in God's Church—to remember that the Church is only as strong as the families (no matter what shape or size) who reside within it. Remember Peter Benson's declarations that I quoted in chapter 1: "As the family goes, so goes the future of the Church. Religious life in the home is more influential than the Church."

As I write this chapter, I'm attending one of my favorite conferences. It's a conference for the senior pastors and their spouses of the large churches (500 or more worshipers) in our denomination, which I attend each year. What makes this conference so valuable is not the keynote speakers we bring in (we don't bring in any), the great worship team that we listen to (we don't have one), or the list of incredible workshops we can attend (we don't have any workshops either), but just the fact that it gives us an opportunity to meet and share our faith journeys with one another.

At the conference, we talk about how God is growing and changing us as leaders. Then, during the next three days, we simply have an open agenda in which we discuss anything we want to discuss. We make a list of topics on a whiteboard and get through as many of them as we can over the next few days. Each year, I'm amazed with how many incredibly valuable insights I glean from peers who minister in similar contexts.

Here's what made the list of topics this year:

- What's happening in our denomination
- Leading from the second chair
- Staffing trials and tribulations
- General board/elder structures
- Transitioning a church

- Closing the back door
- Good books we've read
- Multi-site venues
- Maintaining personal spiritual balance
- What's hot
- Sermon series ideas
- Coaching tips

As you can see, there were a number of important items that made this list and became our topics of discussion. But do you see what didn't make the list? Faith at home. Nor has it made the list in the past four years I've attended this conference. And remember, this is my favorite conference to attend.

The point I'm trying to make is that faith at home isn't even something we're discussing as senior pastors. It's not on our radar. It doesn't make our Top 10 list. Until it does, nothing will change.

When the Senior Pastor Doesn't Lead

As I speak to groups about faith at home ministry, I frequently hear two questions: (1) How can I help my senior pastor recognize our church's need to become faith at home driven? and (2) Can I lead this movement even if my senior pastor isn't on board? Let's tackle the first question first. Here are a few ideas:

- Have your senior pastor read this book. That's why I wrote it! And don't just ask your pastor to read it, but go through it with him or her. What strikes a chord? What doesn't?

- Give your senior pastor a copy of *Transforming Children into Spiritual Champions* by George Barna. Get together with your pastor once a week to discuss each chapter until you complete the book. If you offer to buy breakfast or lunch, you'll have a great chance of success!

- Survey the teenagers in your church to find out how many talk about faith with their parents. Ask them if they have prayer time in their families, family devotions, times of Bible reading and acts of Christian service in the home. Give this information to your pastor. Often, pastors are unaware of how poorly their church is doing with faith at home. Once you've made your pastor aware, he or she will become very interested and open to reexamining things.

For the second question on leading this movement even if your senior pastor isn't on board, I would like you to read what pastor Dave Teixeira wrote on this matter for the *Take It Home* implementation guide:

Would it be great if the senior pastor was on board with your vision to empower families to live out the faith in their homes? Yes.

Would it be great to have sermons about the importance of investing in our children frequently come from the pulpit of your church? Definitely.

And would it be nice to feel like the children, youth and family budget and staffing were a high priority to the leadership of your church? Absolutely.

But here's the deal. I know that Pastor Mark says, "It's critically important for the senior pastor to embrace the idea of becoming a church of family ministry." But the truth is that this might or might not happen. Furthermore, you might not have any control over this.

I'm here to tell you that you can do it anyway. Yes, little old you—the one with the half-office in the back corner of the church basement. I hate to say this, but my co-author is a senior pastor, and to tell you something you already know, they can be a bit narcissistic. They think if they don't start it, support it or promote it, it won't happen. I love you, Mark, but that's not always true . . .

Now, I'm not urging you to do anything in secrecy or even under the radar of your pastor. However, even without your pastor doing cartwheels, you can begin to move forward. Just let the appropriate people know that you're going to start some training events for families, and then get started. Start small, build a team of people with a similar passion and watch things grow. In a few years, when enough momentum has grown, I can assure you that the senior pastor will get on board (and probably take all the credit for your work)!

While I take exception to Dave's comment about senior pastors being narcissistic, the rest of what he says is true (especially the part where we take credit for your work!). This movement can begin without your senior pastor's complete buy in or support. Or perhaps better stated, you don't need to wait for your senior pastor to "get it" before you begin making it happen. In fact, don't wait! Make it happen for the sake of the people in your church who are struggling to live for Christ at home. Eventually, your senior pastor will come to understand the importance of faith at home. Someday, I believe it will even make the list at that senior pastors' conference I love!

2. Make Faith at Home a Part of the Church's Mission

In a compelling talk titled "Four Things You Must Do," Bill Hybels, founding and senior pastor of Willow Creek Community Church, shared that one of the things people need most today is a clear and compelling vision. Hybels illustrated this with a story of a man from another church:

I'll never forget a conversation I had with a churchgoing business guy. He had a huge heart for God at one time, but his heart for God was shrinking. He was in total frustration, and his frustration was leaking out all over the place. He pulled me aside at a conference and said, "Bill, will you meet with my pastor?"

I said, "What for?"

And he said, "To tell him to put a target on the wall. Any target on any wall! People like me just need some direction, some reason, any reason for staying in this game. I'm dying here. I'm dying here."

And he was. He was perishing for lack of a vision.[3]

Target Practice

When a church decides to become a faith at home-driven church, a clear vision has the potential to unite and ignite your congregation. Remember, a faith at home focus affects and engages everyone. A lot of church visions perish because they don't ground the vision through a faith at home set of lenses. The vision might be good, but it can't flourish because it hasn't been driven *home*—literally!

On the other hand, when a church adds the faith at home component to its vision, it becomes a vision that people can see, understand and apply to their own lives. This engages each individual personally in the vision. As a senior pastor, I love it when God provides something that creates unity, engagement and positive momentum in my congregation!

Every church has a mission, vision and/or strategy. For some, it looks like a baseball diamond. For others, it might be five Gs, four Cs, or some other creative acronym. If your church wants to be a faith at home-focused church, that goal must appear in your overall mission, vision and/or strategy.

When I came to Ventura Missionary Church, the leadership had already identified "family" as one of their core values. This was critically important for me, because it demonstrated that VMC understood and embraced the critical role of the family in passing on faith to our children. As a result, when the pastoral team and I went to work creating a new mission, vision and strategy, we did so with family ministry already on our radar.

Take a look at how our faith at home commitment has been woven into our mission, vision and strategy statements: "The mission of Ventura Missionary Church is to introduce people to a growing relationship with Jesus Christ." Our vision, which guides us toward accomplishing our mission, is to continually invite people to:

- *Come and see* what a growing relationship with Christ has to offer you and **your family**.

- *Follow me* and make an **"as for me and my household we will serve the Lord"** decision to enter into this growing relationship with Christ.

- *Go and be* the light of Christ **in your home**, community and world.

As you can see, faith at home is not in the mission statement itself, yet it is woven into our vision and overall strategy for accomplishing our mission. I do not believe that faith at home needs to be in your mission statement itself. A mission statement, in most cases, is a very clear, concise statement of purpose usually driven by Matthew 28. However, I do believe that faith at home must be a critical component of the strategy you have for fulfilling the mission God has given to your church.

For example, as Ventura Missionary Church seeks to introduce people to a growing relationship with Jesus Christ, we believe a growing relationship with Jesus Christ can be defined by four things:

1. Loving and following Jesus Christ
2. Living out faith at home
3. Becoming connected and engaged in the church
4. Making a difference in the community and world

We believe that a growing relationship with Jesus Christ occurs when people are loving and following Jesus Christ and living out their faith at home as well as when they are connected and engaged in a church and using their gifts to make a difference in the community and world. At VMC, we developed an "Are You in a Growing Relationship with Jesus Christ?" checklist that we use to help evaluate and assess where the people are that God brings to our ministry (see appendix 4). We redesigned our website, vmc.net, to then serve as a tool that people could use to help them grow in the areas in which they needed to grow.

If people need help praying or reading the Bible in their home, our website can provide them with tools to help them do this. If they don't know what their spiritual gifts are, our website can help them discover their gifts and find ways they can use their gifts to serve either at VMC or in our community. We want everyone that God brings to us to have a growing relationship with Jesus Christ. Faith at home is an integral part of that mission.

While this isn't particularly revolutionary, it's still significant because it drives home what we do at church. Faith at home is an integrated part of how we do church, and it even impacts the way we set up our website.

3. Commit Resources to Family Ministry

Jesus said, "For where your treasure is, there your heart will be also" (Matt. 6:21). We can easily adapt this verse to apply to the church as well: "Where your budget is, there your commitment as a church will be also." If the church is going to make a significant impact on what's happening in the home, we must commit equally significant resources from our church budgets to staffing and resourcing faith at home.

Unfortunately, in most churches we spend a large percentage of our budget on programs and resources that primarily get used at church but hardly any funds on resources that the family can use in the home. I challenge you to look at your current church budget and ask yourself, *How much money are we spending as a church to equip the home to be the primary place where faith is nurtured?* If the home is more influential than the church, shouldn't we be devoting more resources to what is more effective and God-ordained?

When I served as the youth and family ministry pastor at Calvary Lutheran Church, we spent as much money on resources that we gave away at Take It Home events for families to use in the home as we did on Sunday School curriculum. Let me state that again! *We spent as much money on resources that we gave away at Take It Home events for families to use in the home as we did on Sunday School curriculum.* Obviously, this constituted a major commitment that took many years to build up to.

When I came to serve as senior pastor of Ventura Missionary Church, I knew that we would have to increase our financial commitment to family ministry. On the Sunday that I preached the "Home as Church, Too" message, I painted a picture of some of the steps we would take to equip parents to pass on the faith to their children. I also told the congregation that these ideas needed financial support that wasn't in our budget.

I concluded the message by giving the congregation a chance to make an above-and-beyond financial gift to our new faith at home effort. The congregation responded by giving more than $30,000. This became the seed money we used to fund our new family ministry efforts until we could build it into our annual budgets.

I know that church budgets are tight. But I also know that people will give to a ministry that they sense will make a difference. If you cast a faith at home vision and attach to it the practical resources you need to help families reestablish the home as the primary place where faith is nurtured, the resources will come. In fact, I've discovered that it's easier to get funding for your faith at home movement than just about any other item in your church budget!

Thinking Outside the Box

I've consulted with churches that don't have the funding to get started. Some simply add a faith at home line item to their budget, listing an amount that covers the costs for the resources they want to provide. The pastor and leaders then challenge the church to increase the budget by that amount.

Another approach is to launch a faith at home campaign. Much like a building campaign, with this approach people commit to giving a certain amount to fund a faith at home makeover program. One church I know of did a "bring the light home" campaign. They raised all the resources they needed to fund their faith at home movement for three years! In fact, to date, every single church that I've urged to tackle this issue has been able to raise the resources they needed to fund their movement.

My point is that funding faith at home should be at least as important as any building program you might lead. What if your next capital campaign for a building program also set aside a portion of the funds for your faith at home movement?

We need to think outside the box—beyond our church build-ings and programs—when it comes to our resources.

4. Staff Your Faith at Home Movement

Let's take a moment to discuss staffing your faith at home movement. Perhaps this isn't currently an issue, because you serve in a one-pastor church. However, these principles, while targeted at a larger church, can still be helpful to you if you lead a smaller church.

To be honest, the larger your church is, the more difficult it becomes to be a faith at home-driven church. Why? Because the larger the church becomes, the more specialized the staff becomes, and the more specialized the staff becomes, the hard-er it is to get them all on board. In a larger church, you have to convince a whole team of leaders—who each specializes in an area—that they need to buy into this movement. When you try to become a church *of* faith at home, you need to get all of these specialists on board. This can be an arduous task, because each specialist has a sense of "I know how to lead my area, so don't come in and tell me what to do." Of course, you'll need to han-dle this attitude carefully, yet firmly.

Overcoming the Challenge
One of the best things that a church can do to establish itself as a faith at home-driven church is to hire a children, youth and family ministry pastor. Often, this simply means redefin-ing one of your associate pastor positions. (A children, youth and family ministry pastor's job description can be found in appendix 1.)

The role of the person in this position is to basically pro-vide vision and direction to the children, youth and family min-istries of the church. In many ways, this individual serves as the glue and connector between various ministries. He or she continually asks, "What are we doing? Why are we doing it? How does it connect to the home?" Or, as I mentioned in chapter 4, this person more pointedly asks, "Is what we're doing transferring into how people live at home?"

The individual in this role is recognized as a full-fledged pastor of the church who preaches regularly and oversees the faith at home movement. This person must have a passion for faith at home, and probably also needs to have some experience working in the field of children's or youth ministry. The children, youth and family ministry pastor needs to be a gifted communicator and accomplished leader who works effectively with teams and strong personalities. In many ways, this position provides a great training ground to be a senior pastor one day.

The person in this position doesn't directly lead any ministries, but he or she oversees the staff directing them. In addition, this person serves as another resource to each of these ministries. This pastor also interacts with other areas of ministry and staff members who lead those ministries, ensuring that faith at home becomes an emphasis in every ministry and program of the church.

The children, youth and family ministry pastor also has the power to remove employees who want to continue to work in their "silo" or who adopt a Pied Piper approach. Pied Pipers are usually gifted in working with children or teens but simply don't have the interest or desire to bridge their ministry to the home. Through their dynamic and charismatic leadership, they're able to draw a crowd of students to follow them. Yet in many cases, Pied Pipers see parents as a disruption to the work they're trying to do. Unfortunately, they don't realize that their success or influence is only temporary, and sometimes these leaders need to be removed from their positions in order for the faith at home vision to succeed.

I recognize this won't be easy. I've had to fire employees who didn't buy in to a faith at home vision and tried to maintain their rogue programs. However, if a children, youth and family ministry pastor is going to succeed in helping you become a faith at home-driven church, that person must be able to surround himself or herself with like-minded leaders.

Seeing the Bigger Picture

I strongly advocate for this staff position because without it, each ministry to children and youth can easily become a self-sustained world with its own vision, rules, guidelines and activities. When this position doesn't exist, it's not unusual to have a church send out three mailings promoting six events that all take place in the same week—some on the same night! It's easy for departments and department leaders to get so wrapped up in what they're doing that they lose sight of the big picture. The next thing you know, your church is adding to the chaos most families already face on a daily basis.

I'll never forget when a parent came up to me and said, "Does anyone coordinate what's going on at that church? This week, I received five mailings and I have to try to figure out a way to take my kids to three separate events taking place at three different times on the same day."

A children, youth and family ministry pastor intentionally pulls the team together and coordinates what the church does with children, youth and families—all while looking through the lens of faith at home. This person is an advocate for his or her team members, continually lifting up the value of faith at home through sermons and leadership.

At first, other staff members might be threatened by this new "boss." However, over time, the team members will begin to appreciate the fact that they now have a "go to" person who will listen, advise, counsel and direct them on decisions they need to make. If possible, I would also advise that your church provide this pastor with a communications director for the entire children, youth and family ministry department of your church. This person is not a secretary—he or she is responsible for coordinating all incoming and outgoing communications, registrations, and so forth. Once other team members accept the need for this position—which again will take time because each area previously had the freedom to do it themselves—it will greatly strengthen your faith at home ministry through coordinated communications.

At Calvary Lutheran, we hired a communications director who single-handedly made us a stronger and more effective ministry. Instead of three different mailings going out, she created a children, youth and family newspaper that went out monthly. It not only promoted events but also provided faith at home ideas and articles. She handled all event registrations, which enabled parents to register their children for multiple ministries all at the same time. She also helped us to look at our calendar of events through the eyes of our families. Many times, this prompted us to cancel some events.

Becoming a church committed to bringing Christ back into the center of every home means weaving a faith at home focus into your mission, vision and strategy as well as staffing for it. In many cases, the combination of a children, youth and family ministry pastor along with a communications director provides the winning combination a larger church needs to unite ministry specialists around a faith at home vision.

Adapting in a Smaller Church

If you're in a smaller church where many of your ministries are led by volunteers, I suggest finding a lead volunteer—someone who clearly has a faith at home vision and passion—to oversee the volunteers directing your nursery, children's ministries and youth ministries. Keep this key volunteer free from leading any of those ministries so that he or she can pull together the leaders of those ministries once a month for the purpose of asking, "What are we doing? Why are we doing it? How does it connect to the home?"

Even as a volunteer, this individual needs to be empowered to be the final authority on decisions regarding your faith at home focus. In addition, if this volunteer is looking for more to do, urge him or her to create a children, youth and family newsletter that lifts up all the ministries of your church and provides faith at home activities that parents can do with their children.

5. Get All Ministries and Programs Involved

One common mistake that inhibits faith at home from getting the traction it needs to flourish occurs when churches pigeonhole the movement as family ministry and place it under the umbrella of children's ministry. Unfortunately, this is a movement breaker, because it ends up adding a huge responsibility to an already overextended area. It also prevents other ministries from taking an active role in transforming families.

When your church appropriately elevates faith at home to being a part of how you do church, it becomes something that every ministry can get involved in. Limiting family ministry to children's ministry is a disservice to your families and your church.

Often I'm asked, "How do we get all of our ministries to commit to being a church *of* family ministry?" One of the best ways I've discovered to foster broad support of a faith at home focus is to hold a one-day family ministry summit meeting. (A family ministry summit meeting outline can be found in appendix 2.) The purpose of this meeting is to share the biblical mandate for faith at home as well as to create a sense of urgency, ownership and buy-in for *all* the ministries of your church.

You might see the buy-in that results in very simple and small ways. For example, in one congregation where I served, our family ministry summit meeting led to our men's ministry making faith chests.[4] These wooden boxes, which look like small hope chests, were given to the parents of each child being dedicated. Not to be outdone, the women's ministry gave nighttime devotional tapes to parents on the one-year anniversary of the child's dedication, and the quilting group made baby quilts for each child. The singles ministry decided that they wanted to give Bibles to the family of each third-grader to help parents pass on a tradition of memorizing Scripture to their children. The youth ministry team decided to put together a retreat to help parents and teens talk about dating, kissing and sex.

The family ministry summit meeting can serve as a catalyst for your church's journey toward becoming a church *of* family ministry, as each ministry assumes a part to play in making the vision happen.

6. Preach Faith at Home

This final movement maker or breaker is seen in how your set of faith at home lenses affects your preaching and teaching. Unfortunately, many pastors simply set aside one Sunday a year for a family-focused service or sermon. Some might even go as far as having a family-focused sermon *series* each year, thinking this will challenge families to bring Christ into their home.

I'm sorry to be the one to point this out, but one sermon or sermon series a year will not get the faith at home job done any more than telling your new puppy one time to quit "tinkling" on the carpet! (My mother-in-law uses the term "tinkling" because it's less offensive than the other word.) Just as training a puppy takes a lot of repetition, so too does the consistent reinforcement of faith at home through your preaching and teaching.

Instilling faith at home requires ongoing repetition. Therefore, each sermon you give should have an eye toward how the godly truth, attribute or insight you're preaching about can be transferred into the way people live at home. This doesn't have to be difficult. For instance, you could include in every sermon an at-home application point or could craft your sermon notes in a way that added a few "take home" questions or "when you get home" activities. Sure, this might add 5 to 10 minutes to your preparation time, but wouldn't it be worth it?

When your preaching and teaching becomes ignited with the faith at home focus, you'll continue to fan the flame of family ministry week after week. This will greatly increase your chances of igniting the type of fire for Christ that you want to see in every home. Remember, religious life in the home is more influential than the Church.

Movement Maker or Movement Breaker Key Questions

1. Is your church ready to make a long-term commitment to faith at home while recognizing that there's no quick fix for the transformation that needs to occur within families?

2. Is your senior pastor committed to making family ministry one of the top priorities in your church?

3. Is faith at home integrated into the mission, vision and strategy of your church?

4. What percentage of your budget is committed to providing resources families can use in the home? Is that enough to get the job done?

5. Are all the ministries of the church incorporated and committed to your family ministry efforts?

6. Is faith at home a consistent emphasis in your preaching and teaching?

CHAPTER 6 SUMMARY:

- Connecting the dots: How you can lead a faith at home movement in your church.

- A faith at home-driven church starts with the pastor's personal commitment.

- The leaders of your church need to be as committed as you are.

- Becoming a faith at home church takes a long-term commitment.

- The importance of having extended leadership's buy-in.

- How to stir faith at home passion in the church body.

- How you can sustain and maintain a faith at home focus.

- The messenger is the message.

- Others who've tried—and succeeded!

- Prayer for pastors and churches.

How Do We Connect the Dots?

The entire faith-at-home movement is not about programs, numbers, or facilities. It's about Jesus. Nothing more. Nothing less.

Dick Hardel

Remember connect-the-dot worksheets? When I was a child, I loved connecting the dots. I found something almost magical about how a page of dots could slowly form into a clear image as I methodically connected the dots in order. I loved connect-the-dots so much that sometimes I would take a plain sheet of paper and randomly place dots all over the page. Then I would start connecting the dots to see if an image formed on its own. Obviously, this wasn't as successful as preprinted worksheets. But either way, I found myself entertained and enthralled by connecting dots.

Often, when I attend a conference, sit down with an innovative leader or read a book full of ideas and concepts, I inwardly find myself saying, *Would someone please connect the dots for me?* I love random thinkers, but only for so long! Eventually, I need time to process what they're saying so that I can connect their ideas to my reality.

This was usually the case whenever I sat down with Dr. Dick Hardel, director of the Youth and Family Institute. He could put a thousand faith at home dots on the wall in less than 30 minutes, but he never connected them! Usually, he just looked at me and said, "That's your job. Have fun!" To be perfectly honest, that's why we made a good team—he loved to throw dots on the wall, and I loved connecting them.

So in this final chapter, I want to help you connect the dots for leading a faith at home movement in your church. Just to be upfront, even after we've connected the dots, the image will still be a very big picture without a lot of detail. You'll need to add that yourself, because no two churches are the same. However, we can connect the dots and provide a basic outline that you can then customize and add detail to base on your ministry context.

So let's get started connecting dots!

Dot 1: Make a Personal Commitment

The journey to becoming a faith at home-driven church begins with you, the pastor. God has called you to serve your congregation and to lead it faithfully. Every day, I'm humbled that God chose me to lead a church, because I know that I'm not qualified to do so. I'm in full agreement with the apostle Paul when he wrote, "I am less than the least." I'm a work in progress, and each day seems like another day of training and growth.

I don't know how you ended up with this book in your hands, but God does. Somehow, God placed this book in your hands "for such a time as this." Be assured that he did so for a reason, because that's simply how God works. With Him, there are no accidents or coincidences. He has a plan and purpose for you as a leader, and He'll use books, conferences and other leaders to influence you in the direction He wants to take and grow you.

As a pastor, perhaps you didn't realize the grave situation that exists when it comes to how people live out their faith at home. If so, that's okay, because now you do. The good news is that you can do something about it! You can start by putting on a permanent set of faith at home lenses that will color—in a positive way—the way you lead your church. With this new set of lenses in place, you'll learn to base success less on numbers, programs and buildings and more on bringing Christ and

Christlike living into the home. You'll remember that Jesus was, is and always will be the answer every person and family needs to succeed. Unfortunately, Jesus has been standing outside the home for too long. It's time for us as pastors to help usher Him into the center of every family again.

There's a great painting by Raphael titled *Jesus at the Door*. It depicts Jesus standing at a door, knocking. A vine winds around the doorway, making it appear that the door hasn't been opened for some time. I've heard that when Raphael first showed the painting, a critic pointed out that the artist had forgotten to paint a handle on the door. The painter simply replied, "I didn't forget, the handle is on the other side of the door."

We have a God who stands at the door of our homes knocking. He has always been there, and He will wait there until we let Him in: "Here I am! I stand at the door and knock. If anyone hears my voice and opens the door, I will come in and eat with him, and he with me" (Rev. 3:20).

The faith at home movement begins when we as pastors understand that our role is to help usher Jesus into the center of people's hearts and homes. As Dr. Dick Hardel shared with me, "The entire faith at home movement is not about programs, numbers, or facilities. It's about Jesus. Nothing more. Nothing less."

Where are our eyes as pastors? Are they on the building across town that we wish we had? Are they on the latest and greatest program we wish we could implement in our churches? Are they on the worship leader we wish we could hire? Or are they on Jesus, who stands at the door of every home knocking . . . knocking . . . knocking. He patiently waits for someone to hear Him and open the door so that He can come in and transform that person's and that family's life.

Are you helping the people God has given you to hear Him knocking and to open the door for Him to come in? That's our primary focus. Nothing more. Nothing less.

Dot 2: Bring Church Leadership on Board

Now that you've put on a set of faith at home lenses, the next dot that needs to be connected is to the leadership of your church. The leaders of your church need to become as committed to the faith at home movement as you are. They need to understand the crisis that families are in, recognize the need to bring Christ and Christlike living into the home, and embrace the changes that need to be made to become a faith at home-driven church.

Frankly, one of the mistakes I made during my first years at Ventura Missionary Church was to not take the time to help bring the leaders of the church to the place where I was. I understood the reality and the need when it came to families, had a huge sense of urgency driving me, and recognized what we needed to do to become a faith at home-driven church. But I didn't take the time to make sure the church's leaders saw the need and vision as clearly as I did.

Kurt Bruner, executive director of the Strong Families Innovation Alliance and pastor of Spiritual Formation at the 10,000-member multi-campus Lake Pointe Church in Rockwall, Texas, recently shared with me a process he led his church through that helped create ownership and support from his church leadership for the faith at home movement that he was planning to develop.[1] Kurt is an incredibly gifted strategic thinker and planner who spent 20 years working at Focus on the Family and was also the co-founder of the Heritage Builders Association. (Thank you, Kurt, for allowing me to share your planning process with others!)

The first thing that Kurt did to bring his church leadership on board with the need to become more faith at home-driven was to help them understand their current "as is" reality. He used statistics like the ones shared in this book along with personal surveys from his congregants to help his leadership to see that evangelical churches (especially Lake Pointe) have been highly innovative in reaching the outer rings of the target while assuming the inner ring to be all right. However, the statistics tell us that we can no longer assume the inner ring is okay.

Now that Kurt had the leadership's attention, he then cast a compelling vision for a new reality that he wanted them to move toward. For example, Lake Pointe's vision was to create a model of how a local church could help families build thriving marriages, introduce children to God and increase the odds that those raised in the church would remain in the faith. With this vision in sight, Kurt then asked the team to critically assess their ministries through the lenses of this new vision. For example, Kurt asked questions such as the following:

- What do we currently measure to keep family health and faith formation on our "radar screen"?
- What qualitative measures do we have as examples of how we measure impact versus participation?
- What do current measurements communicate to Lake Pointe staff/volunteers about our priorities?
- What ministry programs at our church intentionally strengthen families?
- What is the approximate participation as a percent of weekend attendance?
- What ministry programs at our church help parents disciple their own children, and what is the approximate participation as a percent of attending parents?
- What is the current process/experience for a family unit at Lake Pointe?
- Do we tend to handle families as a unit or as a collection of individuals?
- Does our current approach drive integration or disintegration of the family faith experience?
- Do we have a single, clear point of entry for a family unit to plug in?

Now that the team had a clear "as is" picture, Kurt turned his attention to helping the team to capture "could be" dreams. In an open brainstorming session, Kurt unleashed the team to come up with outside-the-box ideas of things that Lake Pointe could do in the future in order to . . .

- Give young singles a vision for marriage/family
- Strengthen existing marriages
- Inspire parents to become intentional at home
- Equip parents to pass the faith
- Partner with parents in passing the faith
- Strengthen the parent/teen relationship so that kids want their parents' faith
- Help families experience God as a unit rather than as isolated individuals
- Leverage family focus to attract the unchurched to Lake Pointe
- Create a culture of family-centered faith at Lake Pointe

As the momentum built up, Kurt then worked with the team to draft a "might be" prototype with elements they would need to launch a faith at home initiative that included three key objectives, a core process for family impact, leveraging for existing programs and new concepts to launch. To help trigger their brainstorming, Kurt asked them to complete the following statements:

- We want to move 100 percent of Lake Pointe families from ___ to ___ within 12 months.
- We want to infuse this emphasis into our core programs as follows . . .
- We want to align or adjust our existing programs as follows . . .

- We want to make family core a part of every ministry strategy by . . .

With the prototype now in place, Kurt used the team to nail down "should be" objectives and formalize a "would be" plan. By the time the process was complete, Kurt had involved his leaders in the process, and as a result they were now invested in making the vision happen.

I encourage you to take the time to bring your church leadership on board and not shortcut the process. Big leadership decisions lie ahead, and your leaders need to be united with you in this.

Dot 3: Make Your Commitment Long Term

You can't change your church overnight, so you must make a long-term commitment to becoming a faith at home-driven church. You and your leaders can only establish this long-term commitment if you intentionally do three things that I mentioned in chapter 5:

1. Weave the faith at home commitment into your mission, vision and strategy as a church.

2. Begin devoting funds to provide the resources necessary for the movement.

3. Provide dedicated staff leadership (or, in smaller churches, volunteer leadership) to equip the home to be the primary place where faith is nurtured.

When I look at that list, I realize that none of these steps looks quick or easy. That's another reason why it's so important to have the leadership of your church on board.

Weaving faith at home language into your mission, vision and strategy might be relatively easy, or it might mean you need to do some significant reworking. In some cases, the mission, vision and strategy of a church had been established for years and the idea of changing it in any way is a scary proposition. If that's true in your church, ask yourself and leaders of the church if your mission, vision and strategy truly addresses the faith at home crisis facing families today. Again, you probably don't need to throw out everything you are currently doing. You might just need to tweak things a little to make your mission, vision and strategy even better!

Raising the initial funds and growing your budget to support your faith at home movement over the long haul will also take leadership. You probably don't have funds in your budget to start providing resources to every family in your church in order to equip them to be faith nurturers in their own homes. So I encourage you to devote a Sunday to making a faith at home appeal in which you focus on many of the points we've covered in this book, including:

· The reality that Christlike living is not happening in homes today
· The role that the Church has played in enabling this to happen
· How you intend to reclaim homes for Christ through a comprehensive faith at home strategy (give examples of the type of resources you want to provide for Take It Home events)
· The need for this to happen

Once you have cast the faith at home vision, make the appeal to your congregation and set a big goal! Then give people an opportunity to respond to everything you have said. If all goes well, this kind of faith at home appeal will provide the start-up resources you need to launch the movement. Keep in mind that you'll still need to fund your faith at home movement on a permanent basis through your annual budget. Hopefully, the faith at home appeal will give you a couple of years until the church budget can support the movement on an ongoing basis.

When we launched the faith at home movement at Ventura Missionary Church, we were able to raise more than $30,000 to get started. We eventually began to examine our annual budget and even started to divert resources within the budget to support the Take It Home resources we provided to families on an ongoing basis. Each year, the children, youth and family ministry budget has grown, and now it's the largest part of our church budget. Remember, as Jesus said, "For where your treasure is, there your heart will be also" (Matt. 6:21).

Finding the right staff person or volunteer to provide oversight and leadership to the faith at home movement in your church can also take time. You might discover that the right person is already on your staff and all you need to do is simply rework a job description to give that individual the authority needed to lead the movement. Or you might find that you need to make some difficult decisions in order to staff this movement appropriately. I can't stress enough the importance of finding the *right* person to lead this movement in your church.

John Maxwell, who some call America's expert on leadership, boldly proclaims, "Everything rises and falls on leadership."[2] Just a few simple words, but vital advice. So I urge you to invest in the person who will lead this movement in your church. You probably won't find someone with a lot of experience, because we're at the very beginning of this new movement that God is leading. So look for a person who has the heart, passion and gifts to lead. (For help with this, see the children, youth and family ministry pastor job description in appendix 1). Then invest in this leader by sending him or her to training events and conferences to meet with like-minded people leading the movement in other churches.

Choosing the leader for the faith at home movement in your church is so critical that you might need to make some difficult decisions in order to put the right person in place who can lead the movement forward successfully. For example, when we made faith at home one of VMC's top priorities, our church had a preschool, a K to 8 school, a children's ministry and a youth ministry. Each of these ministries operated in its own "silo," and the leaders had never been pulled together to think or work as a team. We knew that becoming a faith at home-driven church meant that we needed to hire a pastor to oversee this team and drive the movement.

Unfortunately, in order to accommodate this new leader, we had to eliminate another pastoral position. One of the hardest days I've ever had as a pastor was the day I had to tell a very committed and caring pastor who had served VMC faithfully for more than 15 years that his position was being eliminated. To this day, I'll never forget his gracious response: "As hard as it is to hear this, I want you to know that I think you made the right decision." In the months that followed, God provided for this pastor to continue to serve and use his gifts in a church in a neighboring community. Although this decision was difficult, it was the right decision for the long-term future of VMC and the commitment we had made.

I would like to say that everything was rosy after that. However, after we hired our youth and family ministry pastor, we discovered that people on our team didn't share our faith at home commitment. We had to make more changes—which weren't any easier. In fact, it took almost three years to get to the place where the church had a united faith at home-driven youth and family ministry team. But now we're there, and we're never going back!

(How awesome is this—another "God thing" just happened. I'm writing this chapter in an airplane coming back from a conference in Florida, listening to my MP3 player to block out external noise. The instant I finished the previous paragraph, FFH sang the following line: "Through it all, I'm in it for the long haul." I believe God is trying to tell us something!)

While becoming a faith at home-driven church begins with you as the pastor, it will require you and the church's leadership to make some decisions that will prove that this commitment is real and long term. If you make the changes I've described, your church will remain a faith at home-driven church whether you stay there or not.

As pastors, we need to take the passion we have to see Christ in the center of every home and transfer it into the very DNA of the church. This takes time and fortitude. However, the hard work you put in now to become a church *of* faith at home will keep your church on the right course for generations to come! Even if transferring your faith at home commitment takes a few years, it will all be worth it. Remember, "Religious life in the home is more influential than the Church."

Dot 4: Foster Extended Leadership's Buy-In

The next dot that needs to be connected is for the extended leadership of your church to engage in your faith at home movement. The Faith at Home Leadership Summit outline in appendix 2 can help you foster buy-in from the leaders of all the ministries of your church.

I'll never forget the first Leadership Summit that Dave Teixeira and I led at VMC. To be honest, it was the first time all the leaders of the ministries of the church— including the leaders of our men's, women's, children's, youth, adult, small groups, missions, and other ministries—had ever met in the same room together. Dave and I shared with them some basic statistics about the state of families, including the reality that less than 10 percent of the families in most churches truly have Christ and Christlike living in the center of their homes.

We also gave a very abstract vision for how we could become a faith at home-focused church. Then we asked what they thought.

The response was overwhelming! Each leader shared how faith at home was the primary stumbling block he or she was facing. The idea of coming together to work collaboratively on the problem was something each of them couldn't wait to start. We began laying out our Take It Home events. When the meeting concluded, we had a plan to launch eight Take It Home events in the first year and to add five more the following year.

Even more important than this plan was the infectious and contagious spirit that developed among the leadership of the church. We all saw where we were heading and understood the role we would play in helping to make our congregation a faith at home-focused church. In following years, the summit became a time to share success stories, hear testimonies of lives that had been changed, review and revise the plans for the upcoming year, and share ideas for the future. From that first leadership summit meeting on, we moved from being a church *with* a family ministry to a church *of* faith at home.

The logo you see grew out of one of our Faith at Home Leadership Summits. Our children, youth and family team created it to represent VMC's faith at home movement. This logo appears on literature sent out from our children, youth and family ministries. I also use the logo in our new member classes and with visitors to describe our commitment to be a faith at home-driven church. (Feel free to use this logo or create something yourself to represent the commitment your church is making to focus on faith at home.)

Dot 5: Stir Passion in the Church Body

Another dot you'll need to connect pertains to the people who faithfully attend and serve your church body. Over time, a church takes on the passion and personality of its leader. The people of your church will become passionate about what you're passionate about. As you become a faith at home-driven pastor, you will need to stir the same passion in your church.

One way to share your outlook is through a sermon series. As I mentioned earlier, one sermon series a year isn't enough to keep the faith at home movement alive in a church. However, one sermon series is definitely enough to launch the movement and create a sense of urgency and expectancy in your congregation. In the *Take It Home* implementation guide, Dave Teixeira and I outline a five-week sermon series that can serve as a good movement launcher for congregations. Such a sermon series will give your congregation the opportunity to see your passion and commitment. It can start the faith at home ball rolling and give the movement a push that will continue gaining momentum for years to come. (One word of caution: Be careful not to preach this kind of sermon series before you're ready to launch the movement, because people will be ready to respond. Remember, even if they're not aware of it, they've been waiting a long time for something like this!)

Another way to engage your congregation is to spotlight the Take It Home events you've started. Keep your congregation aware of what your church is doing to bring Christ and Christlike living into the home. Show the resources you give away at each Take It Home event. This allows the people of your church to see how families are using the resources they've been providing.

In one church where I spoke as a guest, the pastor placed a faith chest on the stage and slowly filled it with all the resources the church would provide through their Take It Home events during the year. The pastor explained each resource and how it would help the family in the home. When he was finished, he thanked the church for its faith at home commitment and for the funds they had provided to help make Take It Home events happen. This visual illustration conveyed to the people just how serious the church was about equipping the home to be the primary place where faith is nurtured. As the pastor finished, I remembered thinking, *I'm going to do that in my church!*

Dot 6: Maintain Momentum

The final dot you need to connect is the "maintaining the momentum" dot. As with any new movement, the leaders and members of your church will have a lot of passion and excitement in the beginning. But over time, their attention and focus might wander and they might lose some of their commitment and drive.

Remember that a faith at home focus requires a long-term commitment. Your church must stay the course for the next 20 to 30 years and beyond! While programs might have life cycles, this isn't just another program. Here are a few suggestions for how you can keep the faith at home ball rolling.

First, at a leadership level, make sure that your evaluation of both paid and volunteer leaders includes the impact that their ministry is having on your church's faith at home movement. How is their ministry helping instill faith at home? How are the people they minister to becoming more faith at home driven? What influence has their ministry had on faith at home? When your ministry leaders realize that faith at home is part of how their job performance will be evaluated, they'll be sure to focus their attention on the home instead of what happens at church.

Another way to keep the movement moving is to continually add and strengthen Take It Home events. The Take It Home strategy you implement will continue to evolve and get better over time. Pastor Dave Teixeira describes it this way:

What just happened? I thought as I left church that morning. I never thought I would get my rear whooped by a bunch of two-year-olds, but I just had. It was our first Take It Home event for two-year-olds and their parents on family blessings. We had a great morning planned, with food, music, a puppet show and even a little set portraying a child's bedroom where we would show parents what blessing your child each night before bed might look like.

Feeling like the parents would want some Bible exposition on the theology behind blessing, I had come prepared with about 10 minutes of teaching on the subject before we got practical and began helping parents write and practice blessing their own children. For some reason (and this is surprising, because at the time I had a two-year-old), in my mind the two-year-olds were going to sit quietly in Mommy's or Daddy's laps while I talked peacefully with the parents about the history and theology of blessing. You know what happened instead. Kids were everywhere. Moms were up and chasing. Dads were frustrated, and I literally could not get through one sentence without a major interruption. I felt like we had failed.

But here's the point: We hadn't failed! First of all, several parents from that group told me later that they had begun blessing their children, and one father told me that his daughter won't go to sleep without his blessing her first. (Again, the goal isn't focused on how the event goes!) Second, and most important, we had learned. Following the event, we went right to work evaluating and brainstorming how we might change the format for next time to help things run smoother. And you know what? It did.

This year, we tried our first Computer Savvy Parents Take It Home event for parents of middle school and high school students. It was okay. Honestly, I gave the event a D+ (I'm a hard grader). However, I promise you that next year's event will be better, because we learned so much this first time. During Q&A, we learned what kinds of questions parents will ask. Watching parents and kids interact, we discovered where the tension points between parents and kids lie. We found out how much time it takes to do a virtual tour of the Internet and what parents want most in terms of filtering info. So, despite our D+ this year, the event was a success and a step in the right direction. Next year, I'm anticipating at least a B.[3]

I love what the family ministry team at VMC comes up with for Take It Home events. The resources they find and the events they provide continually amaze me. My own family has been blessed through the Take It Home events we've had opportunity to participate in. Each year, the church adds a few more. The events we continue to offer seem to get stronger each year. The members of this team have a long-term vision and commitment! They recognize that these Take It Home events aren't something the church does for a season but that they make up a permanent part of how we do our ministry to children and youth and whole families. The team is continually looking for ways we can improve our Take It Home strategy, and they consistently look at resources, visit other churches and attend conferences. As a result, our faith at home focus gets stronger and better each year.

That leads to the final way you can maintain momentum: Affirm positive behavior. When you see or hear how a ministry has made a faith at home shift, no matter how subtle it may be, affirm that change! Nothing means more to paid staff and volunteers than hearing an affirming word from the pastor. Because the move to becoming a faith at home driven church is a gradual process, you'll need to gently support your leaders.

Will there be failures and misses? Absolutely. I could fill at least another chapter with all the mistakes and misses I've had through the years. But at least we were trying, and in every situation we learned something that made us better the next time around. Even when your leaders attempt something and fail, affirm them for trying. Not every attempt will succeed, and that can kill momentum unless you affirm the attempt. Often, that's all a leader needs to keep on going.

Will This Really Work?

Throughout this book, I've told many stories about myself and the churches where I've served. I've shared how we implemented a vision, mission and strategy to bring Christ and Christlike living back into the home. I've stuck my neck on the line a bit to tell you about my own experiences, because when it comes to the faith at home movement, I believe that the messenger is the message. I've tried to give you a glimpse of how God has used and blessed me by allowing me to be at the leading edge of this important movement.

Of course, you might be thinking, *Sure, the faith at home way of ministry works for you, Mark, because you've helped lead it. But I don't see how it could work in my church.* Before you dismiss it all, I would like to remind you of the crisis families are facing. In chapter 1, I shared some startling statistics with you regarding the state of faith in the family. Let's review those briefly here. In Search Institute's national survey of more than 11,000 participants (churched youth) from 561 congregations across 6 different denominations:

- Only 12 percent of youth have a regular dialog with their mother on faith/life issues.
- Just 5 percent of youth have a regular dialog with their father on faith/life issues.

- Less than 1 in 10 (9 percent) of youth experience regular reading of the Bible and devotions in the home.
- Just 12 percent of youth have experienced a servanthood event with a parent as an action of faith.[4]

Researcher George Barna confirms these results: "In a typical week, fewer than 10 percent of parents who regularly attend church with their kids read the Bible together, pray together (other than at meal times) or participate in an act of service as a family unit. Even fewer families—1 out of every 20—have any type of worship experience together with their kids, other than while they are at church during a typical month."[5]

Again, I believe that Christ is not pleased with the state of families or how the Church has enabled families to get into this state. I hope you see that as a church leader, you and your church have a job to do. It's as simple as that. And, yes, you can do it! As I said before, it doesn't matter what size church you serve. It doesn't matter whether you pastor a mainline, evangelical, traditional, postmodern, build-the-believer or seeker-oriented church. It doesn't matter if you're Lutheran, Catholic, Presbyterian, Assemblies of God, Baptist, Evangelical Free, non-denominational or any other label or non-label you want to put on yourself. You and your church have a job to do—a holy job that Christ calls you to!

While becoming a faith at home church isn't just a program in a box that you can implement as is, I hope you've learned how to put on a set of faith at home lenses that will change the way you lead your church. We all face the same truth—the home is the primary place where faith is nurtured. Period. The question is, Will we accept the job that God wants us to do?

Others Who've Tried—and Succeeded

To encourage you that your efforts will be successful, I would like to close this chapter—and this book—with just a few notes

I've received from leaders whose churches have committed to equip homes to be the primary places where faith is nurtured.

Tim Coltvet
Mt. Olivet Lutheran, Plymouth, Minnesota

As we begin to prepare for the coming year, our church has become increasingly convinced that we need to identify faith in the home as a core strategic principle.

This past January, we decided to invite Mom and Dad to the church building for our junior high program nights. We were pleased to have you as guest speaker for one of these events. With the sanctuary full of junior high students and parents, you laid the foundation for a meaningful conversation with our families. You began the journey by asking us a question: "What would it look like for your family to have an extreme home makeover . . . with Christ at the center?"

After this event, our church began to ask volumes of questions and to carry on hours of discussion about our congregation's ability to ensure that future generations would carry with them and pass on faith in Jesus Christ. As we continued the discussion, we slowly realized that this concept was becoming a part of the DNA of our congregation. By the end of our January session, our senior pastor was so moved by the data and critical nature of the discussion that he urged the church council, staff and congregation to help envision and continually embrace a "faith in the home" philosophy in our congregational life.

Exactly what's being born within our congregation, I can't be sure. But it's clear to me that the Holy Spirit is working to redefine the way we pass on the faith in the twenty-first century. Shame on me, as a pastor, for thinking that my sermons on Sunday morning should be the primary arena for faith formation and growth in a young person's life. Now we know from research that a simple question from Mom or Dad like "Where did you meet God today?" will have a much more profound effect on the faith formation of that child.

In the words of another friend of mine, "It's time to alter the home with a home altar." We're completely on board with this vision, and we're seeing our families come to life as they embrace their critical callings for God's kingdom.

Gary Strudler
Rolling Hills Community Church, Portland, Oregon

Just a quick note to let you know that our Home Court Advantage classes with parents and kids are going extraordinarily well. Parents and kids have been excited to get the one-on-one attention, and parents walk away with some practical helps and resources to help them be the spiritual leaders they desire to be. We made the jump from three classes last year to providing an event for each grade level this year! Thanks, Mark, for allowing the Lord to use you to speak to people like me! Faith at home was exactly the direction our church wanted and needed to go. It's also amazing that I've been able to share it with other children's leaders in our area.

From Lynn Adams
Lighthouse Missionary Church, Elkton, Michigan

In 2005, I was introduced to George Barna's book *Transforming Children into Spiritual Champions*. Through that book, God gave me two major visions for ministry. First, we must stop running programs and become deliberate about making disciples who make disciples. Second, we must help parents own the responsibility of training up their own children to be disciples, with the help and support of the Church. At that time, I really thought it would be a hard sell to parents, but I started sharing the vision personally and publicly.

In answer to prayer, God raised up a team of 10 people—including our senior pastor—to attend the Healthy Home Initiative seminar, where many heard you share your faith at home vision.

After the seminar, I called together those who had attended. My purpose was twofold: (1) to find out what they had learned, and (2) to come up with some goals to work toward in our local church. They were very enthusiastic, and some wanted to start Take It Home events at every age level within the year. In reality, things have moved a little more slowly than that. This team, with a few others, formed a new Family Ministries Council and has met every month since that time.

Our senior pastor, other members of the council and I have all shared during church services the truth that training up children to be disciples needs to be our top priority. We started a family newsletter, which introduces two family units each month in order to help families get to know one another and also highlights a specific book or resource that parents have found helpful in training up their children. The team also divided the church families into seven groups, with each couple on the team committed to praying faithfully for the spiritual health of families in their group over the course of the month.

We also developed a master schedule that lists the Take It Home events we'll introduce over the course of the next three years. In the meantime, we've paired up multiple age levels so that more families can participate sooner.

I'd like to take this opportunity to thank you for being faithful to share the burden God has laid on your heart. It has certainly changed the way I look at ministry and the way we do things at Lighthouse Missionary Church.

Jean Perdu,
Oakridge Presbyterian Church, London, Ontario
Your main sessions and breakouts on faith at home ministry at the Navigating New Waters: Children's & Family Ministries conference brought walloping confirmation to the thoughts

and prayers of our team. You put into words what we'd been grasping for and gave us spiritual foundations and practical ideas for putting those thoughts into action. We left knowing that God had some new plans for us, but we also left feeling like we'd been trying to take a drink from a fire hydrant!

Not wanting to lose a single drop, our team quickly focused in on the "key learning" from each session. We reviewed our materials and began to plan. Knowing it wasn't possible to implement everything, we focused on small changes that would make a big difference. Our team prayed and planned and launched our "Family Zone: Building Faith in Families" ministry.

We desire to see children grow to be adults who love the Lord their God with all their heart, soul and mind and to love their neighbors as themselves. We've made it our goal to equip, empower and encourage families to grow in their faith and pass it on to the next generation. A group of woodworking men has become involved and have been building faith chests for each child, which parents receive when their infants are baptized. The chests are meant to hold a child's spiritual keepsakes as well as the resources they'll use to "cut" their spiritual teeth on. The idea is for each child to have a chest filled with faith building tools to pass on to their own family.

We also implemented faith builder workshops this year for three of our age groups with more in store for next year. These workshops take place during Sunday service times, and parents attend with their children. Each workshop focuses on a specific faith tool and provides children and parents with teaching, application and resources to continue honing that faith tool in their daily lives.

We're thrilled to see all that God has done with our new faith at home focus in less than a year. From this impact, our congregation has a nearly audible buzz, which continues to grow as we eagerly anticipate what God will do next!

A Hope and a Prayer

I hope you're seeing how each church that puts on the set of faith at home lenses begins to see their unique situation differently and how each congregation determines how to change their vision, mission and strategy with their new faith at home focus. I believe that this approach works so much better than a program in a box, because it stirs a deep passion within the people of each church.

Let me share my prayer for you as we close:

I pray God will personally give you the desire to have your church become a place that equips the home to be the primary place where faith is nurtured and that He will help you make a personal commitment to lead a faith at home-driven church. Further, I pray that God will work through you to bring your church leaders on board—to become as committed as you are. I pray that together, you'll see the importance of making this commitment long term—to last long beyond when all of you are enjoying old age or life with Jesus in heaven! And I pray that you'll be able to stir passion in your church as you share how the faith at home vision will influence, in a positive way, every member of your church as well as generation after generation to come!

Children, Youth and Family Ministry Pastor Job Description

by Dr. Dick Hardel[1]

Youth and family ministry is a new paradigm that has a focus on faith formation. Some congregations have begun to use new titles for this position of leadership. Some new titles are: minister to the Christian home, director of faith formation, director of faith nurture in the home, or director of discipleship in the home. These new titles are used to move the members of the congregation away from the old paradigm of youth group or youth ministry separated from the whole ministry of the congregation.

From the study of research on faith formation, The Youth and Family Institute has shared that the home is the primary place to teach and nurture faith. The congregation is in partnership with the home and works to strengthen the adults in the home to pass on the faith. In this new paradigm, a director of youth and family ministry must work with the parents and other primary caregivers as well as the children and youth of the congregation and community. This ministry must be built from a new vision, rather than around the personality of a person.

At our institute, when we talk about youth ministry, we mean from pre-birth to about age 35. It is about passing on the faith and nurturing the faith. When we talk about family, we do not mean one specific type of family. We mean working with every type of family to grow in Christ. This includes single adults. Their family may be made up of two or three very close friends who share faith, values and friendship. That also is family. Family goes beyond immediate blood relatives and includes mentors, friends and others outside the household.

Often, when a congregation seeks to fill a part-time position in youth and family ministry, it is because the congregation cannot financially afford a full-time position. However, the expectations of the leadership of the congregation often equal that of a full-time position.

Since the concept of youth and family is a new paradigm, it may be difficult for a congregation to find a person who is trained in this new model. My first suggestion is to search for someone who has the heart and the call for ministry. It may be someone from the congregation. Our institute, the Center for Youth Ministries at Wartburg Seminary, and a few other organizations provide continuing education and critical skills courses in youth and family ministry. This is an option to consider and may be easier than trying to locate someone outside of your congregation with the passion and skills for this ministry.

Key Attributes of a Director of Youth and Family Ministry

1. Loves the Lord and can express his/her faith well
2. Loves the Church
3. Loves to be with children, youth and their families
4. Is a director and not just a doer
5. Understands ministry as team
6. Is willing to receive coaching, outside training and on-the-job training
7. Faith is founded in a theology of the cross (grace-oriented), and lives a faith-filled and faithful life in response to God's grace. In other words, this person models the gospel of Jesus, the Christ.

Everything else can be taught. But the attributes listed above are essential.

Other Essential Things to Consider

- *Understanding Youth and Family Ministry:* Youth and family ministry is a holistic and intergenerational approach to ministry. It is primarily not about children, youth or families. It is primarily about Jesus. It is about discipleship and passing on the faith. It is not just children's ministry or youth ministry. It is everything that God is doing in the community through the congregation. Thus, a director of youth and family ministry must work with the whole ministry team of the congregation, have a clear understanding of the vision and mission of the congregation and understand faith formation.

- There are four imperatives in youth and family ministry:
    1. Faith-focused Christian education
    2. Strengthening family relationships
    3. Congregation as family
    4. Christian youth sub-culture

- There are four keys to nurturing faith in the home:
    1. Caring conversation (includes faith talk)
    2. Devotions in the home
    3. Family service (in the neighborhood and community)
    4. Rituals and traditions in the home

- The congregation must offer a salary so that the director can raise a family and stay for many years.

- The congregation should financially support the ongoing training of the director of youth and family ministry.

- The director of youth and family ministry must know how the congregation is structured and functions.

- The job description must clearly state that the director of youth and family ministry is to equip and mentor parents and other adults as well as youth with leadership skills to do the ministry. The job is to build on God's vision, equip families for their ministries, direct the ministries and support the doers of ministry.

- For the health and wellbeing of the director of youth and family ministry and the longevity of the ministry, the director of youth and family should develop strong, spiritual disciplines (i.e., personal prayer, devotional life, daily reading of Scripture, faithful and regular attendance at worship, and develop a prayer support team).

- The director of youth and family, as with all other members of the ministry team, is accountable to the vision of what God is doing in and through the congregation. All the ministries in youth and family ministry must connect to the vision of the congregation.

- The director of youth and family ministry should develop a discipling ministry of leadership for both youth and adults in the congregation and community.

- The congregation should develop a clear plan for future growth of the person and the position. It is helpful to find a coach for a person in a new position.

- The congregation's budget for youth and family ministry must reflect a good salary with benefits, support for the planning and carrying out of ministries, and continued education of staff and other lay volunteers to be trained.

Faith at Home Leadership Summit Outline

by Mark Holmen and Dave Teixeira[1]

This outline for holding a Faith at Home Leadership Summit has been reprinted from the *Take It Home* implementation guide, published by Gospel Light. Corresponding Power Point slides for the highlighted items are available as a part of the *Take It Home* implementation guide.

I. Opening: Create an Inviting Atmosphere
   A. Food, decorations, music playing, name tags, etc.
   B. Have people sit at round tables in their ministry teams. For example:
      1. Table 1—Music and worship leaders (lay and staff)
      2. Table 2—Adult ministry leaders (men's ministry, women's ministry, etc.)
      3. Table 3—Children's ministry leaders
      4. Table 4—Youth ministry leaders
      5. Table 5—Elders/general board
   C. Begin by thanking people for giving their most precious commodity—their time—to participate in this summit meeting.

II. Time of Worship (30 minutes)
   A. Take time to refuel your leaders through a time of praise and worship.

B. Pray for the Holy Spirit to come and give your team unity and vision for a family ministry that will transform the lives of families in your community.

C. Add your own worship slides.

III. Session I: What Are We Accomplishing? (60 minutes)

A. *Opening discussion starter*: Before we get started, an important point to note is that when you use the word "family," you are talking about every form of family. A single person in a nursing home is a form of family, a dual income no kids (DINK) couple is a form of family, etc.

1. Tell the audience that a *USA Today* article once stated that there were over 28 forms of family.

2. State that when you say the word "family," you will be talking about all 28 forms of family.

3. Share the following quote from Peter Benson, Director of Search Institute: "As the family goes so goes the future of the church. Religious life in the home is more influential than the church."

B. As a group, discuss the following questions:

1. How are families in our church and community going today?

2. If this is the future of the Church, what does that mean for our church?

3. Do you agree that religious life in the home is more influential than the Church? Why or why not?

C. In a national survey by Search Institute titled "The Most Significant Religious Influences," teenagers were asked to identify what factors influenced them to have faith. Their answers were quite revealing:

1. Influence #1—Mother

2. Influence #2—Father

3. Influence #3—Pastor

     4. Influence #4—Grandparent

     5. Influence #5—Sunday School

     6. Influence #6—Youth Group

     7. Influence #7—Church Camp

     8. Influence #8—Retreats[2]

D. But the key finding was that Mom and Dad were two to three times more influential than any church program!

E. How is religious life in the home today? Have the participants guess the answers to the following Search Institute survey of more than 11,000 participants from 561 congregations across 6 different denominations. Remember, these are the responses from churched teenagers!

     1. What percentage of teenagers have a regular dialogue with their mother on faith/life issues? (12 percent)

     2. What percentage of teens have a regular dialog with their father on faith/life issues? (5 percent)

     3. What percentage of teenagers have experienced regular reading of the Bible and devotions in the home? (9 percent)

     4. What percentage of youth have experienced a service-oriented event with a parent as an action of faith? (12 percent)[3]

F. Share the following quote from George Barna: "We discovered that in a typical week, fewer than 10 percent of parents who regularly attend church with their kids read the Bible together, pray together (other than at meal times) or participate in an act of service as a family unit. Even fewer families—1 out of 20—have any type of worship experience together with their kids, other than while they are at church during the typical month."[4]

G. Discuss together the following questions:

    1. Based on these statistical realities, how is religious life in the home today?

    2. What do you think has caused this reality?

    3. What has the church done or not done to cause or address this reality?

H. Let's hear what others are saying (share the following quotes):

    1. "For all their specialized training, church professionals realize that if a child is not receiving basic Christian nurture in the home, even the best teachers and curriculum will have minimal impact. Once-a-week exposure simply cannot compete with daily experience where personal formation is concerned."[5]

    2. "When a church—intentionally or not—assumes a family's responsibilities in the arena of spiritually nurturing children, it fosters an unhealthy dependence upon the church to relieve the family of its biblical responsibility."[6]

    3. "Most certainly father and mother are apostles, bishops, and priests to their children, for it is they who make then acquainted with the gospel."[7]

    4. "Most teenagers and their parents may not realize it, but a lot of research in the sociology of religion suggest that the most important social influence in shaping young people's religious lives is the religious life modeled and taught to them by their parents."[8]

    5. And finally, my favorite quote from Dr. Roland Martinson of Luther Seminary: "What we ought to do is let the kids drop their parents off at church, train the parents and send them back into their mission field, their home, to grow Christians!"

I. Let's look at one other source: the Bible!
   1. Have someone read the following passages:
      a. Deuteronomy 6:1-12
      b. Joshua 24:14-16
      c. Psalm 78
   2. Discuss how faith at home is a biblical mandate!
J. Review: What have we discovered?
   1. Religious life in the home is more influential than the Church.
   2. Mom and Dad are two to three times more influential than any church program.
   3. Yet faith talk, devotions, Bible reading, prayer and service aren't happening in the home.
   4. Faith at home is biblically mandated and what God intended.
K. Conclusion: Therefore, we need to get religious life, Christ and Christlike living back into the center of every home!
   1. Close with the following quote from Mark Holmen: "I believe one of the greatest existing challenges facing the Christian Church today is trying to figure out how we can equip the home to once again be the primary place where faith is nurtured through our existing ministry structures."
   2. State that this will be the focus of our next session.
L. Take a 30-minute break.

IV. Session II: Becoming a Valuable Partner (minimum 2 hours)
   A. Open with the following quote from George Barna: "The local church should be an intimate and valuable partner in the effort to raise the coming generation of Christ followers and church leaders, but it is the parents whom God will hold primarily accountable for the spiritual maturation of their children."[9]

B. Discuss the following together:
1. Is your church currently a valuable partner in bringing Christ and Christlike living into the home?
2. Do unchurched people recognize your church as a valuable partner for them as parents or as a program center for their kids?
3. Does your church have any of the following symptoms:
    a. An increasing number of parents who simply drop their children/youth off for the programs of the church but never attend themselves?
    b. A decreasing number of students attending or participating in the programs of the church as they get older?
    c. An increasing number of students and/or young adults who abandon their faith as they get older?
4. If your church has any or all of these symptoms, you're not alone. These are the symptoms of a church that has focused on having great programs and leaders who engage people at church but at the same time has gotten away from making the home—and Mom and Dad—the primary influencers of faith development.
5. Let's take a look at *how* we can equip the home to once again be the primary place where faith is nurtured *through* our existing ministry structures.
C. Go through the family ministry vision and "Church of Family Ministry" model found in chapter 3.
1. Go through the add-a-silo versus church *of* family ministry models as explained on pages 77-80.

2. Discuss what it means to become a church *of* family ministry versus a church *with* family ministry.

3. Tell the audience that you are now going to focus the rest of your time together on *how* to become a church *of* family ministry.

D. The five keys for becoming a church *of* family ministry:

1. Key #1—the commitment of the senior pastor

a. Ask your senior pastor to share his/her passion and commitment for becoming a church *of* family ministry.

b. How has God put this vision on your pastor's heart?

2. Key #2—a part of the mission/vision/strategy of the church

a. Do your church's mission, vision and strategy accurately reflect your commitment to be a church *of* family ministry?

b. What changes could/should you make?

c. How will these changes be shared with the congregation?

3. Key #3—involve all the ministries

a. State how each ministry of the church, represented here today, has a role to play in the church becoming a church *of* family ministry.

b. Go through and explain the Take It Home events listed in chapter 3 and how these can serve as the backbone for your faith at home initiative as a congregation.

c. Give each ministry 30 to 60 minutes to discuss what they could do to help make the faith at home movement happen. Questions they should discuss include:

i. How can we contribute to becoming a church *of* family ministry?

    ii. How can we partner with our people to bring Christ and Christlike living back into the home?

    iii. What Take It Home event(s) could we initiate or help make happen?

    iv. Is there another ministry we should partner with to help make this happen?

  d. Bring everyone back together and list the ideas each ministry came up with on a whiteboard.

  e. Organize the ideas by establishing the dates and times for each Take It Home event.

  f. Determine who will provide the leadership for each event.

4. Key #4—commit the resources necessary

  a. Does the church have the resources that will be needed to make this initiative happen?

  b. Are there any additional funds/resources that will be needed?

  c. How will those funds be secured?

5. Key #5—make a long-term commitment

  a. In many ways, to become a church *of* family ministry requires a "back to the future" type of commitment. We're not going to change families overnight, but we do need to change families by reestablishing them and their homes as the primary place where faith is nurtured.

  b. George Barna describes it similarly: "Christian families taught the ways of God in their homes every day. Parents were expected to model a Spirit-led lifestyle for their children, and families were to make their home a sanctuary for God. In a very real sense, the home was the early church—supplemented by larger gatherings in the Temple and elsewhere, but never replaced by what took place in the homes of believers."[10]

E. Closing the session

    1. Conclude by stating that today was the beginning of a long-term work that God wants to do in and through you as a church.

    2. Celebrate the fact that you now have the beginning framework for your faith at home initiative that will influence and transform families for years to come!

    3. Commit the decisions that were made to prayer.

    4. Close by sharing the date for next year's summit, where you will evaluate and add more layers to your faith at home initiative.

Frequently Asked Questions

As I travel across the country and even around the world sharing the faith at home movement with pastors and church leaders, these are some of the commonly asked questions I receive.

Q. Is this just an issue in the American Church?

A. Absolutely not. I recently spoke to a group of international church leaders from 13 different countries. When I finished, the response and desire from these leaders to have the faith at home movement brought to their countries was overwhelming! I've learned that the program-driven model is clearly established in Christian churches around the world, which also means there is a need for faith at home to exist all over the world. I wonder if this is one of the reasons why house churches are becoming increasingly popular and effective. House churches are naturally all about faith at home! Maybe we should learn from them.

Q. What if people resist or outright reject the idea of faith at home because they simply want an experience they can come to or a place where they can drop off their children?

A. I've never liked this question, because it forces us to do something we don't like to do: choose. "But if serving the Lord seems undesirable to you, then choose for yourselves this day whom you will serve, whether the gods your forefathers served beyond the River, or the gods of the Amorites, in whose land you are living. But as for me and my household, we will serve the Lord" (Josh. 24:15).

I've found that the majority of people will embrace a faith at home movement, especially when they experience Take It Home events for the first time and realize how serious a church has become about helping them as people and families to establish Christlike living in the home. Most people want to be healthier and stronger spiritually. So when a church provides ways to help them be healthier and stronger, they're both surprised and elated.

Still, some people will always simply want the "professionals" to do it for them. They don't want the church to ask them to do anything more or to change anything about them or their way of life. They just want to drop off their kids so that the church can teach the faith and instill good values in their children while Mom and Dad head to the health club or supermarket.

At Ventura Missionary Church, when we are confronted with this situation, we simply tell people that we may not be the right church for them. When I meet with visitors and every new member class, I clearly let people know that if they're looking for a church where they can drop off their children and expect us to teach them the faith, we're not the right church for them.

As pastors and church leaders, we have to make a choice. Is faith at home important or not? For me, I've decided that this is a non-negotiable matter. So we let our people know that. And then, by the way we structure our ministries, we show them that faith at home is a non-negotiable matter.

Q. What if the parents don't show up for the Take It Home events?

A. I would like to say that we had 98 percent turnout from the first day we offered a Take It Home event, but that wouldn't be accurate. Over a few years, we've grown to the place where we have this kind of turnout by offering the Take It Home events through our normal Sunday School or youth ministry programs and by making sure the events are valuable and equipping. Still, we do have a few children who show up without parents. So, what do we do with them?

First, we ask them where their parents are. Many times, the parents simply forgot about the event and went to the worship service. If that's the case, we actually go and get the parents out of the service. In fact, I've even made the announcement, "If you're the parent of a second-grader who is enrolled in our Sunday School, you need to go and join your child at his or her Take It Home event that is taking place now in room . . ."

If we can't locate the child's parent, we then ask the Sunday School teacher of that class to serve as a surrogate parent for that event. This teacher encourages the students to do the faith skill with their parents when they get home, and the teacher also calls the parents after the event to explain the faith skill that the children learned to do with their parents at home. In most cases, these parents are the first to show up at the next Take It Home event the following year!

Q. How do you incorporate new families who join the church and have missed previous Take It Home events?

A. In most cases, the family can simply start where they are and move forward. For example, if a new family comes to our church with a teenage daughter, we won't start by trying to teach the parents how to start blessing her each evening. Her first Take It Home event might be the "Dating, Kissing, Sex and Stuff" retreat, where we help the parents and teen to have a shared experience and discussion about these critically important issues.

Would it have been beneficial for this family to have experienced the previous Take It Home events and to have learned how to pray together, read the Bible together, and so forth? Absolutely. Yet each Take It Home event is a targeted, age-specific event that doesn't require participation in previous events. In many cases, a family will ask us if they can have some of the resources or ideas we shared in previous Take It Home events. We gladly make those resources available.

Q. Will the older generation support this movement?

A. In a word, yes. The bigger question is will the church include them in the movement. Senior adults need to be included in faith at home because of the vital role they can play. Some ideas for incorporating seniors into a faith at home movement include "meddling grandparenting" workshops. In these events, the church intentionally equips the senior adults to be faith mentors in the lives of their grandchildren. The church can also start a faith-mentoring program to build relationships between the senior adults and students.[1] In addition, the church can include senior adults in Take It Home events for testimonies or as church grandparents who simply participate with the families.

Q. How do you incorporate or take single people into consideration?

A. Singles need faith at home as much as married people. For example, I've been asked to bless the apartments of single adults in my congregation, which becomes a powerful testimony that they're going to make sure Christlike living happens in their home. This is an amazing commitment for a 22-year-old to make when a more natural temptation might be for him or her to have the apartment be a party place. It is important for the church to include singles in the discussion about faith at home and also ask them how they can help make the single's ministry more faith at home driven. You'll find that many of them appreciate this change in focus.

In addition, the church should invite people in its singles ministry to engage in and even lead Take It Home events. At VMC, our singles ministry decided to put together a Halloween "monster mash" event for parents and children to attend as an alternative to trick-or-treating. The singles group provided all the leadership for the event. Families that attended were blessed as their children participated in a safe, faith-nurturing family event on Halloween.

Q. Who do you turn to for ideas/resources for your movement?

A. The first answer that comes to mind is *everywhere*. Our church's family ministry team and I are continually looking for ideas and resources that can be used at home. We search Christian bookstores, catalogs, websites and anywhere else we can think of to find the most cost effective or free resources possible. Very seldom do we use the same resource for more than five years, because it seems like another resource comes out that's a little better and often a little less expensive.

I also turn to friends who are likeminded in the way they lead their churches. One of my best friends, Tim, is a youth and family pastor. We're frequently calling, emailing or getting together just to share ideas with each other. Proverbs 27:17 says, "Iron sharpens iron," and that's always been the case for me. Tim will take a resource, program or idea and put his faith at home twist on it, and before long I'm applying it in my church. This is the reason we created a faith at home website (www.faithbeginsathome.com)—so likeminded people could share ideas and resources with one another.

Finally, another source I turn to is the Youth and Family Institute. They've been championing this cause from a relatively mainline-church perspective for more than 20 years. You can link to their site from the Faith at Home website. You'll find that they have a lot of resources, training events and ideas that support the movement.

Q. What would you say to pastors in training?

A. First, I would point out that they probably won't receive any faith at home training in Bible college or seminary. So faith at home is a perspective they will need to bring to their training classes or seminars.

This is both a challenge and an opportunity. It's a challenge because their professors won't be prepared for them questioning what they're learning with this perspective. This might create some "we haven't done it that way before" tension. Higher education isn't known for quickly embracing new ways of looking at things. In my own experience, I've found myself running into a brick wall as I try to challenge educators to think beyond the church to the home. They've been looking at things through church lenses so long that it's difficult for them to see things any other way.

However, for pastors in training, this presents a great opportunity to don a set of faith at home lenses as they go through training. I wish I'd had this perspective change when I went through seminary. I would have looked at things differently. I only saw things through a lens of how to teach or apply this at church.

In many ways, pastors in training can get a jump start by putting on a set of faith at home lenses from the very beginning of their calling and career.

Are You in a Growing Relationship with Jesus Christ?

Self-Assessment/Evaluation

Part 1: You Loving and Following Jesus Christ

1. Do you understand who you are in relation   _____
   to Christ?
2. Do you understand who Jesus Christ is?   _____
3. Have you accepted Jesus Christ as your personal   _____
   Lord and Savior?
4. Have you affirmed that decision through Baptism?   _____

Part 2: You Living Out Your Faith at Home

1. Have you established your home as the primary   _____
   place where your faith will be lived out and
   nurtured?
2. Do you have a regular habit of reading the Bible   _____
   at home?
3. Do you have a regular habit of praying at home?   _____
4. Do you have a regular habit of worshiping at home?   _____

Part 3: You Connected and Engaged in the Church

1. Are you worshiping regularly at your church   _____
   (at least 3 times per month)?
2. Are you connected into the church's community   _____
   through a small group or Bible study group?
3. Have you identified what your spiritual gifts are?   _____

4. Are you using your gifts in service to the Body of   _____
   Christ at your church?
5. Are you tithing, or on a path toward tithing, to your _____
   church body?

Part 4: You Making a Difference in the Community and World

1. Are you using your gifts to help people in need   _____
   in your city?
2. Are you engaged in some sort of global missions?   _____
   a. Are you praying for missionaries?   _____
   b. Are you supporting missionaries financially?   _____
   c. Have you participated in a short-term   _____
      mission trip?
   d. Are you feeling called into a long-term mission _____
      opportunity?
3. Are you sharing your faith with others and leading   _____
   others to Christ?
   a. Have you received training in how to share your   _____
      faith with others?
   b. Have you identified three people to whom God _____
      is calling you to be salt and light?

Endnotes

Chapter 1: What Are We Accomplishing?

1. George Barna, *Transforming Children into Spiritual Champions* (Ventura, CA: Regal Publishing, 2003), p. 81.
2. Christian Smith with Melinda Lundquist Denton, *Soul Searching* (New York, NY: Oxford Press, 2005), pp. 188-189.
3. "Number of Unchurched Adults Has Nearly Doubled Since 1991," The Barna Group, May 4, 2004. http://www.barna.org/FlexPage.aspx?Page=BarnaUpdate& BarnaUpdateID=163 (accessed May 2007).
4. Barry A. Kosmin, Egon Mayer and Ariela Keysar, "American Religious Identification Survey 2001," The Graduate Center of the City University of New York, December 19, 2001. http://www.gc.cuny.edu/faculty/research_studies/aris.pdf (accessed May 2007).
5. Cathy Grossman, "Charting the Unchurched in America," *USA Today*, March 7, 2002. http://www.usatoday.com/life/dcovthu.htm (accessed May 2007).
6. *Effective Christian Education: A National Study of Protestant Congregation,* copyright 1990 by Search Institute SM.
7. Barna, *Transforming Children into Spiritual Champions,* p. 78.
8. Marjorie Thompson, *The Family as Forming Center* (Nashville, TN: Upper Room Books, 1996), p. 26.
9. Barna, *Transforming Children into Spiritual Champions,* p. 81.
10. Peter L. Benson, *All Kids Are Our Kids* (San Francisco: Jossey-Bass, 2006), p. 107.
11. Chart on Faith Influence in Youth, reprinted with permission from *Effective Christian Education: A National Study of Protestant Congregations.* Copyright " 1990 by Search Institute SM. No other use is permitted without prior permission from Search Institute, 615 First Avenue NE, Minneapolis, MN 55413; www.search-institute.org.
12. Search Institute is a nonprofit, nonsectarian research and educational organization that advances the wellbeing and positive development of children and youth through applied research, evaluation, consultation, training and the development of publications and practical resources for educators, youth-serving professionals, parents, community leaders and policy makers (see www.search-institute.org).
13. Smith with Denton, *Soul Searching,* p. 56.
14. Larry Fowler, *Rock-Solid Kids* (Ventura, CA: Gospel Light, 2004), p. 24.
15. Ibid., p. 25.
16. Dawson McAlister, *Finding Hope for Your Home* (Irving, TX: Shepherd Ministries, 1996), n.p.
17. Barna, *Transforming Children into Spiritual Champions,* p. 24.
18. Martin Luther, "The Estate of Marriage, 1522," cited in Walther Brand, ed., *Luther's Works* (Philadelphia: Fortress Press, 1962), p. 46.
19. Fowler, *Rock-Solid Kids.* p. 7.

Chapter 2: Do We Care?

1. Mark DeVries, *Family-Based Youth Ministry* (Downers Grove, IL: InterVarsity Press, 1994).
2. George Barna, *Revolution* (Carol Stream, IL: Tyndale House Publishers, 2005), p. 35.
3. DeVries, *Family-Based Youth Ministry.*
4. For information on "The Family Blessing," contact Rolf Garborg at 4090-145th Street, Prior Lake, Minnesota, 55372. Phone: (612) 440-7780.

Chapter 3: What Should We Do About It?

1. Marjorie Thompson, *The Family as Forming Center* (Nashville, TN: Upper Room Books, 1996), p. 144.
2. George Barna, *Revolution* (Carol Stream, Illinois: Tyndale House Publishers, 2005), p. 35.
3. Ibid.
4. Larry Fowler, *Rock-Solid Kids* (Ventura, CA: Gospel Light, 2004), p. 25.
5. Thompson, *The Family as Forming Center,* p. 23.
6. Christian Smith with Melinda Lundquist Denton, *Soul Searching* (New York: Oxford Press, 2005), p. 57.
7. Clyde A. Holbrook, *The Ethics of Jonathon Edwards: Morality and Aesthetics* (Ann Arbor, MI: University of Michigan Press, 1973), p. 83.
8. Barna, *Revolution*, p. 24
9. *Take It Home* implementation guide is published by Gospel Light, Ventura, CA.
10. A complete dedication/infant baptism order of service can be found in the *Take It Home* implementation guide (Ventura, CA: Gospel Light, 2007).
11. The Faith Chest idea is trademarked by the Youth and Family Institute. For more information, including reproducible drawings and plans, go to the Youth and Family Institute website at youthandfamilyinstitute.org.

Working Lunch: Some Insights from a Practitioner

1. John Raleigh Mott, quoted in Gordon S. Jackson, compiler, *Quotes for the Journey, Wisdom for the Way* (Colorado Springs, CO: NavPress, 2000), p. 175.

Chapter 4: How Do We Commit to This?

1. George Barna, *Revolution* (Carol Stream, Illinois: Tyndale House Publishers, 2005), pp. 25-26.
2. Ibid., p. 49.
3. Thom Rainer, *Breakout Churches* (Grand Rapids, MI: Zondervan, 2005), pp. 57-58.
4. Ibid., p. 64.
5. Ibid.
6. Ibid., p. 65.
7. Ibid.
8. Ibid., p. 171.
9. Barna, *Revolution,* pp. 25-26.

Chapter 5: Will We Be Movement Makers or Movement Breakers?

1. Robert Greenleaf, *Servant Leadership: A Journey into the Nature of Legitimate Power and Greatness* (Mahwah, NJ: Paulist Press, 1977), p. 29.
2. Thom Rainer, *Breakout Churches* (Grand Rapids, MI: Zondervan, 2005), p. 58.
3. I heard Bill Hybels deliver this talk titled "Four Things You Must Do" at a Leadership Summit. The talk has been redistributed and is available through the Willow Creek Association's "Defining Moments" series. To order a copy, contact the Willow Creek Customer Service Center at 1-800-570-9812, or visit the Willow Creek website at www.willowcreek.com.
4. Trademarked through the Youth and Family Institute of Minneapolis, MN, www.youthandfamilyinstitute.org.

Chapter 6: How Do We Connect the Dots?

1. If you want to learn more about the Strong Families Innovation Alliance, visit www.strongfamilies.org.

2. John Maxwell, *The 21 Irrefutable Laws of Leadership* (Nashville, TN: Thomas Nelson, 1998), p. 225.
3. Mark Holmen and Dave Teixeira, *Take It Home* (Ventura, California: Gospel Light, 2007), p. 00.
4. ECE study, Search Institute, Minneapolis, Minnesota.
5. George Barna, *Transforming Children into Spiritual Champions* (Ventura, CA: Regal Books, 2003), p. 78.

Appendix 1: Children, Youth and Family Ministry Pastor Job Description

1. Used with the kind permission of Dr. Dick Hardel, Youth and Family Institute, Minneapolis, MN, 877-239-2492, youthandfamilyinstitute.org

Appendix 2: Faith at Home Leadership Summit Outline

1. Mark Holmen and Dave Teixeira, *Take It Home* (Ventura, CA: Gospel Light, 2007).
2. For the complete results, see Mark Holmen, *Faith Begins at Home* (Ventura, CA: Regal Books, 2006), p. 43.
3. *Effective Christian Education: A National Study of Protestant Congregations,* copyright 1990 by Search Institute SM. No other use is permitted without prior permission from Search Institute, 615 First Avenue NE, Minneapolis, MN 55413; www.search-institute.org.
4. George Barna, *Transforming Children into Spiritual Champions* (Ventura, CA: Regal Books, 2003), p. 78.
5. Marjorie Thompson, *Family, the Forming Center* (Nashville, TN: Upper Room Books, 1996).
6. Barna, *Transforming Children into Spiritual Champions,* p. 81.
7. Martin Luther, "The Estate of Marriage, 1522," quoted in Walther Brand, ed., *Luther's Works* (Philadelphia, PA: Fortress Press, 1962), p. 46.
8. Christian Smith, *Soul Searching* (New York: Oxford University Press, 2005), p. 56.
9. Barna, *Transforming Children into Spiritual Champions,* p. 83.
10. George Barna, *Revolution* (Carol Stream, Illinois: Tyndale House Publishers, 2005), p. 24.

Appendix 3: Frequently Asked Questions

1. A faith-mentoring program is included in the *Take It Home* implementation guide I co-authored with Dave Teixeira (published by Gospel Light, Ventura, California).

For more information about the
Ventura Missionary Church, please contact:

Ventura Missionary Church
500 High Point Drive
Ventura, CA 93003
(805) 642-0550

www.vmc.net

More Resources by Mark Holmen

Take It Home
Inspiration and Events to
Help Parents Spiritually Transform
Their Children
Mark Holmen and *Dave Teixeira*
ISBN 978.08307.44572

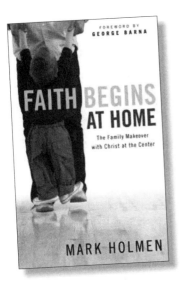

Faith Begins at Home
The Family Makeover with
Christ at the Center
Mark Holmen
ISBN 978.08307.38137

Raise Your Children to Love Jesus

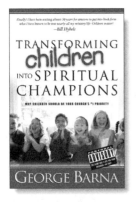

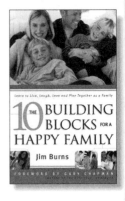

Transforming Children Into Spiritual Champions
Why Children Should Be Your Church's #1 Priority
George Barna
ISBN 978.08307.32937

Rock-Solid Kids
Giving Children a Biblical Foundation for Life
Larry Fowler
ISBN 978.08307.37130

The 10 Building Blocks for a Happy Family
Learn to Live, Laugh, Love and Play Together as a Family
Jim Burns
ISBN 978.08307.3302?

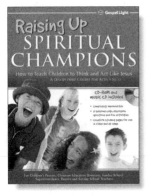

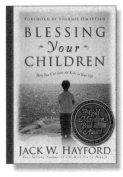

Raising Up Spiritual Champions
How to Teach Children to Think and Act Like Jesus
A Discipleship Course for Ages 9 to 12
ISBN 978.08307.36638

Raising Up Spiritual Champions Newsletter
CD-ROM included
Jean Lawson
ISBN 978.08307.44930

Blessing Your Children
How You Can Love the Kids in Your Life
Jack Hayford
ISBN 978.08307.008491